SECRET SERVICE

BY FRED SIRIEIX

quadrille

PUBLISHING DIRECTOR: Sarah Lav
CREATIVE DIRECTOR: Helen Lewis
EDITOR: Susannah Otter
DESIGNER: Katherine Keeble
COVER PHOTOGRAPHY: Chris Terry
WRITING CONSULTANT: James Steen
PRODUCTION CONTROLLER: Nikolaus Ginelli
PRODUCTION DIRECTOR: Vincent Smith

Published in 2017 by Quadrille, an imprint of Hardie Grant Publishing

Quadrille
52–54 Southwark Street
London SE1 1UN
www.quadrille.com

Text © Fred Sirieix 2017
Design and layout © Quadrille Publishing Limited 2017
Photography © Chris Terry 2017

Cataloguing in Publication Data: a catalogue record for this book is
available from the British Library.

ISBN: 978 1 78713 011 1

Printed in Europe

NOTE TO READERS: some names and identifying details have
been changed.

'EXCELLENCE IS AN ART WON BY TRAINING AND
HABITUATION. WE ARE WHAT WE REPEATEDLY DO.'

Aristotle

To my children Andrea and Matteo Lucien
To my parents Claude and Françoise Sirieix
To my brother Pierre

CONTENTS

FOREWORD

I still remember when Fred started working at Le Gavroche as a young waiter, fresh out of catering college and with a typical French 'I-know-best' attitude. Answering back and being a little gobby can get you into trouble, especially when you're a new member of staff. However, Fred was, and remains, exceptional. Even as a young waiter, his talent was evident and he reinforced this with a boundless drive and energy.

There was never a dull moment with Fred. His speed of thought meant that he was always one step ahead of everyone, which annoyed some of the older members of staff and very occasionally, I had to step in to calm the tension.

Fred was destined for greatness, and he climbed up the ladder at Le Gavroche very quickly. Silvano, our maître d' at the time, immediately saw his talent. Even if a little rough around the edges, it was there, plain for us to see. My father remarked several times how good he was at surveying the room and how professional he was, but he wished Fred would slow down as his perpetual movement was making him dizzy!

Throughout his career, Fred has always given 100% and this book not only gives you a little peek into what makes him tick, but also what makes him so brilliant at what he does.

No longer an employee or a colleague, I now consider Fred a friend. I can't wait to see the next chapter of his life unfold as he still has so much more to give.

Michel Roux Jr, London, June 2017

1

YOU AND ME

Service comes down to one thing: the beat. Like the thump of a drum, the beat follows me during every single service. When things are going well, there's an orchestra playing in harmony with this beat: the happy laughter of customers, the clinking of glasses, the appreciative silence as people enjoy their food. This beat should be inaudible to you, the guest at a table in my dining room, and it is so subtle that sometimes it is even imperceptible to some of my team of waiters and waitresses. It's for me, the restaurant manager, and it is up to me to own the beat from the time the first guest arrives to the moment the last one leaves.

At the beginning of service the beat is slow – a gentle tap, tap, tap. As things speed up, so too does the beat – boom, boom, boom. All I need to do is listen – be sensitive to it – and then I will feel the rhythm of how service should be; if things are off the beat, I can get them back on. Once I have it, I can control the pace. And if I can do that, then I've cracked it.

In the same way that Usain Bolt methodically warms up before the 100m, I have to prepare my staff to move at the right rhythm. So, if there are ten guests, we go at 10km/h, a slow, purposeful beat. If we are looking after 100 guests, well, then we shift up a few gears, and speed along at 100km/h. All this takes preparation and constant attention, in direct contrast to the experience of you, the guest. As the guest, your role is a series of simple pleasures and undemanding questions. What shall I choose from the menu? Shall we have Bordeaux or Burgundy? Who fancies dessert?

For me, as the restaurant manager, there are different questions, and they're a whole lot more complicated. You see, service is like a battle – only the most perceptive and proactive strategist will be victorious. It is the only way. And so I constantly ask questions. When and where are the guests going to be seated? How many guests can I sit at any given time in each station? There must be time to re-set tables once the guests have walked out of the door, and even as more guests arrive. Am I pushing it too hard, and will the team have the time to deliver our high standards and meet the guests' expectations? What reinforcements do I have? Are they trained? Can I pull them out of one position and put them into a new one at a moment's notice? Is everyone briefed? When the battle starts to rage it will be too late to strategise. The thinking and co-ordination must all be completely thought through before service starts. That, as I see it, is the battle plan.

Just as a general watches the brow of the hill to see when the enemy comes into sight, the manager should observe his front door – that is where the 'danger' comes from. That is where you, the guest, will arrive and where we, the hosts, must be prepared. As I need to run the place from the word go, I need to control how guests come to reception. This is completely vital. Reception is where we give guests that crucial first impression. We are all the same: if our first impression is a positive one we are more likely to seek, see and have that same impression of our overall experience. However, a negative first impression has the opposite effect. We will look for and find the bad in everything. You know what they say – if you look for trouble, sure as hell you'll find it. From the door, you can control the flow of customers – because I run the restaurant and the guests do not. But as more guests arrive, the front-of-house staff must beware that the danger can come from any part of the restaurant – people can and do move around. To retain control it is essential that I listen to that beat.

So as a manager, I am always thinking about what is happening now – and what might happen next. My goal is to ensure you have the best possible experience, leave the restaurant happy, and then rave about it to your family and friends. If I do my job well, then to you everything will seem effortless, and the team will enjoy themselves during the 'performance'. This is our Holy Grail: pulling it off is just as hard as finding the real one, because it all has to appear effortless.

The manager who fails to consider how the restaurant will function when it is busy fails to consider the success of his or her restaurant. Nobody wants to walk into an empty restaurant, so it will stay empty. The establishment that is full – or appears full – will bring in more business. The more occupied it is, the more people like it, as long as you run it properly. And where there is business, there is money … then you can reinvest, keep the place looking beautiful, afford to take on good staff, and continue to do this job, day in, day out.

Every day I make a plan and then I wait for the buzz and the beat of service to begin. I try to see everyone and everything as things get busy, and all the time I listen for that beat.

That's how it is for me. How is it for you?

Here you are, on the doorstep of a restaurant.

You have not been here before, but this is a new and trendy place and needs checking out. It may well be an expensive meal, but so what? Tonight is a special celebration. You have dressed up nicely for the occasion. You are just seconds away from starting a great evening. Surely nothing can go wrong. Can it?

You step inside.

There, at the reception desk, is the manager or head receptionist. He is at the computer and at first he does not look up. You see him before he sees you. This is a bad sign. When he does glance up, he does not smile. Big mistake. You have to be the first to say hello. Oh dear. He has not followed the first and most basic rules of service: see, smile and say hello to the guests before they see, smile and say hello to you.

You have booked a table, but when the unwelcoming man at reception scans the list of reservations your name is not there. This is not getting any better, is it? What is worse, he does not seem bothered, and instead behaves like one of those bored flight attendants on a badly run airline who has no interest in customer service.

He takes you to your table. As you follow him, none of the other staff take any notice of you, or make any attempt to welcome or greet you with a smile. Neither does he pull out any of the chairs from the table – a common courtesy that says, 'Welcome. Please sit down and relax. You are special. You are our guest. We are going to look after you.'

At the table, you are left alone with your thoughts – never leave a guest alone with his or her thoughts. These will be thoughts such as, 'When will we be offered a drink? Are they going to bring the menus? Where are the loos, or do we have to ask?' The finest manager, maître d' or waiter – the one who lives for the art of hospitality – can intercept these thoughts, among many others, before they have time to pop into your mind.

So, as you wait for a drink, you take a look at the table. White linen tablecloth, check. But is it creased or, worse, does it have a stain on it? Is the cutlery neatly aligned? Is the knife, fork or spoon – or all three – smeared? Someone has not remembered to polish these items before setting the table. Is there dust on the light bulbs near the table? If you slide your hands under the seat is there chewing gum stuck to it? All these things represent a failure by the staff to pay close attention to detail.

And all of this takes place before you have tasted a morsel of food, or even ordered a dish. Not only that, but in a couple of hours you'll be asked to pay! You are past the point of no return. The food, when it finally comes, won't taste as good as you were hoping for, because nothing leading up to the arrival of the food has been as good as you were hoping for. You, the customer, will be painfully aware of the beats that the staff have missed: from that very first moment when the receptionist failed to see you.

Going to a restaurant is a journey, and along the way there are many touchpoints, from the components of the service to what appears on the plates. To be a good waiter, you need to be completely aware of every single one of these moments. Each and every one should earn a 'Wow!' from the guest. When you have missed more than one, and fail to acknowledge it, alarm bells start to ring in the guest's head. You are in a restaurant where the standards are not high. The will – the desire – to please is missing. It can only go downhill from here, or simply stay mediocre. Either way, you won't be coming back.

Look, I am not saying there won't be challenges. There are plenty of them, but my job is all about anticipation, and I like to give people what they want before they even think of asking for it. There is the 'what' you see, and then the 'what' I see. And often I do not want you to see what I see. I have to see all the guests, and anticipate any problems or disruptions to the beat, before anyone else has noticed.

Guests might arrive inebriated. I would rather you did not see them as it will only spoil the atmosphere. They must be politely turned away. Some might be rude or even aggressive. What matters most in these situations is dealing with them in a way that means not a single beat is missed, and all the other guests carry on, oblivious.

I remember four men, in their mid- to late-twenties, smartly dressed and well spoken. They had seemed all right – steady on their feet, at least – when they came into the restaurant, but looks can be deceiving. From the other side of the dining room, I sensed something was not quite right. The young men had become loud and other guests were starting to feel anxious. Then I saw that there was a plate on the floor. On it was the remains of a main course: a forkful of juicy, rare fillet steak, a sliver of black truffle and a smear of red wine jus. I went to the waiter for the table, and stated the obvious, to try and get a hold on the situation.

'There is a plate on the floor.'

'I know.'

'Okay. You know. Fine. But why is there a plate on the floor? What is going on?'

'Fred, they are very loud. Swearing. The other customers are wondering what's going on and we don't know what to do … And they're very rude men and we just …'

I interrupted, 'But how did the plate end up there?'

'The customer put it there.'

'What?'

Now, the customer is king. Or indeed queen. This means, of course, that the guest can do whatever he or she wants in your restaurant. Unfortunately, a tiny percentage of people are awful. Socrates wrote about the pursuit of virtue, that is, choosing consciously whether to be good or bad. If you are in a restaurant and you put your plate on the floor, this is an act that falls into the 'bad' category. Our freedom ends where someone else's begins. Not only is it bad of you to do this, but it is bad for others. It is bad manners. Who in his right mind would put his dirty plate on the floor when eating at his parents' house? Other guests have come for a special evening and a drunken man who dumps his plate on the floor will spoil the atmosphere and disrupt the harmony of the room. It can threaten the beat and affect the rhythm of service.

I walked over to the table, bent down and picked up the plate from the floor. I maintained a smile. The smile is so important, particularly when you are thinking on your feet and know that you must keep the beat going in spite everyone else. 'Gentlemen,' I said, hushed but audible, 'how are you? Are you having a good meal?'

Four upper class voices replied: 'Yah.'

'Gentlemen, I'm just going to tell you that your attitude at the moment is not right for this restaurant. The people nearby are very worried and I'm here to let you know that. And the fact that you put your plate here,' – I nodded towards the floor – 'is unacceptable. I have picked it up now but if you carry on I will ask you to leave immediately and I will have to call security.'

None of them moved, because they knew, if they moved they'd be out. Just one strike and you're gone. All was calm from then on. Sometimes, in this job, just like in battle, you have to push it a little, though only if you really need to.

You will come to a restaurant to kick back and have fun. These men will have done the same, but they took it too far. As a manager, you must always be on your guard for the people who might do this. Perhaps the most surprising example of this concerns matters of the heart (or the loins). A friend of mine works in a prestigious restaurant in the City of London. Dealing swiftly with people who were getting a little over-amorous became a large part of his job. On one particularly notable occasion, a couple slid off their chairs and began to have sex under the table, not quite hidden by the linen tablecloth. What to do? Well, of course you have to be polite, you have to be in control. So my friend went over to the table, and knocked on it. Knock! Knock! 'Please can you come out? We have other guests in the restaurant.'

This sort of thing isn't common, but it isn't exactly unusual either. Be warned, should you ever feel the urge – resist it. It is highly likely to be captured on the CCTV cameras. I saw a friend in the business the other day. He pulled out his mobile phone and said, 'Have a look at this.' Then he showed me CCTV footage from the restaurant where he works. It showed a man and a woman having a very good time. It was not family viewing, let's just put it that way.

I've had my own brushes with amorous guests. One evening a very well-known footballer came for dinner with a companion. He was a Frenchman like me, and a star in the Premier League. Halfway through the meal, he and his companion left the table and went to the loo. Actually, they went to the same loo – the Ladies – and then into the same cubicle.

They returned about 15 minutes later, and finished their meal. They had certainly worked up a healthy appetite. Funnily enough, the footballer had such a fabulous meal that he returned a couple of weeks later. This time he came through the doorway with his wife. She walked in first, he was behind her, and he looked at me. He raised his two index fingers to his mouth, pleading for a big shush. I obliged, of course – anything for the beat.

2

WHO'S WHO

You are in a decent restaurant with your family and friends, and may well feel like you are the one in charge. Indeed, that is precisely how you should be treated. Behind the scenes, however, there are the real bosses: the people who are looking after you, cooking your food and serving your wines. Each of these people are performing a tightly defined role.

A large, well-organised, high-end restaurant has a strict chain of command, not unlike military ranks. If this does not exist, and staff do not know exactly what they should be doing, the restaurant will fail.

The system most commonly used in restaurants dates back to ancient times when it was used in the kitchens of palaces and castles. It relies on a strict hierarchy, which enables perfect cooperation between the kitchen and front-of-house staff, and was perfected more than a century ago by the great French chef Auguste Escoffier. He introduced the system to hotels across Europe, including The Savoy in London, and it has since become firmly established as part of restaurant tradition. If you're in a well-run restaurant, this is how it will be working behind the scenes.

The hierarchy begins and ends with the *maître d'hôtel*, or maître d': he is the top dog and oversees the restaurant – the waiting staff know not to mess with him. He will be on the frontline, welcoming guests, taking orders as well as constantly keeping an eye on everything else. The guest should always feel like a general, giving the orders, in charge of their own meals, but in fact, to the waiters, the maître d' is the person in charge. Depending on the size of the restaurant, he or she may have one or more assistants, traditionally called *maîtres d'hôtel de carré*.

The maître d' or their second-in-command then gives the order to the *chef de rang*. Now, to the outside world, the chef de rang (or CDR) is not a chef, as he is not in the kitchen – he is a waiter. Depending on the size of the restaurant, there can be any number of chefs de rang. The *rang* is the station – or section – of a restaurant. Each rang consists of 4–12 tables, according to the style of service and the size of the restaurant. So the CDR is indeed *un chef*, as in the French word for a chief or boss – he is the boss of a station.

Having passed the order to the chef de rang, the maître d' can continue to take orders from other tables, and oversee the running of the room. At this point the chef de rang is now responsible for getting the order to the kitchen, and the finished dishes from the kitchen to the tables within his station, therefore freeing up the maître d' to continue attending to the guests. Before service, the chef de rang is also tasked with setting up the tables and preparing the dining room so that it looks beautiful and spotless when the guests arrive.

While the maître d' has the chefs de rang to help him, each chef de rang is also assisted. He has a sommelier (wine waiter), and a number of junior staff. This staff consists of a *commis de rang*, otherwise known as a *commis de salle*, or waiter in plain English, perhaps a *demi-chef de rang*, and a busboy, who is at the bottom of the pecking order. These can all be referred to collectively as 'commis'. The most important part of all these roles is assisting their chef de rang in executing the order, placed by the customer, carefully passed on by the maître d', as smoothly as possible.

—━━

Now let's follow the order as it is passed through to the chefs in the kitchen. The front-of-house staff and the kitchen staff are separated by the pass (or *le passe* in French), which is a kitchen counter: a divide that separates the waiting staff from the kitchen brigade during service. Here, the orders are handed over by the waiter from the dining-room side of the swing doors. The finished dishes are placed on the pass ready to be collected by the waiter. But let's not get ahead of ourselves.

Before we get to the other side of the pass, I will mention a position that not every restaurant has, but one which is close to my heart. In some restaurants (including Galvin at Windows) there is a *chef de passe*. This person is the go-between for the head chef and maître d'. The chef de passe is also known as a *chef de salle* (*salle* being the French for dining room). He communicates with the chef and orchestrates, coordinates and manages the other commis to take the dishes to the dining room (which, in the business, is known as the 'room'). The chef de passe also ensures the back-of-house areas (such as lavatories and storage areas) are always clean and spotless..

On the kitchen side of the pass, facing the chef de passe or another commis will be the *chef de cuisine* or the head chef. At this point the word 'chef' acquires its bilingual meaning of cook. Perhaps he or she is also the chef-patron, or chef-proprietor, who by definition owns or co-owns the restaurant. But whether they have their own share in the restaurant or not, this chef is (or thinks they are) the boss of the kitchen. During service they will check that every single dish is right – indeed, perfect! – before it leaves the kitchen. The chef might even arrange the components on the plate as they are brought up by members of their team. Presentation is vital because, after all, we taste first with our eyes.

The head chef has a *sous chef* (a sort of first lieutenant) or two, depending on the size of the place, and beneath the sous chef, there could be a junior sous chef. Then there are the *chefs de partie*, known in the United States as line chefs or line cooks. They oversee a kitchen section, such as sauce/meat, fish, hot starters, cold starters, or pastry. Pastry, by the way, is not just pastry, but describes the section that makes all the desserts, cakes and those moreish petits fours that are served at the end of a meal with coffee. In some kitchens, you can at times find a *chef tournant*; a jack-of-all-trades chef de partie, who can cook in any section (including pastry!). These guys are rare, they are the SAS of the kitchen.

The chefs de partie usually have assistants, but how many

depends on the size of the kitchen and the number of guests to feed. These assistants are *demi chefs de partie* and then *commis chefs*. The kitchen might also have an apprentice chef (the kitchen equivalent to a busboy, a dogsbody). He or she is usually a teenager who dreams of working up through the ranks. All too often apprentice chefs were pushed around by those above them, who had exactly the same thing happen to them, and thus believed it to be character-building. I am not convinced, but hey, the kitchen is not my domain …

Finally, there is the *plongeur*, the kitchen porter (or KP). He or she does the washing up and keeps the kitchen clean. In larger restaurants you might also find a chef who oversees the larder or pantry, and even a butcher and a baker, but I think that is enough for now.

And so, there you have it. This hierarchical system works very well in maintaining and improving the culture and standards within a restaurant, and there's a reason it has remained unchanged for nearly 150 years. The clear chain of command means that when something does go wrong (and in this business, it will), there is someone to step in, and that person will already have a clear idea of the role they are inhabiting. But it's not perfect – what system is? As is the case in the army, everyone has to follow orders and comply, no matter what. And if you aren't the one giving the orders, then it is likely that at some point you will feel resentment and jealousy, and this can lead to dissension in the ranks.

It has all got a little more complicated over the years. Gone are the 'good old days', when people did exactly what was expected of them, nothing more and nothing less. Integrity and leadership qualities are more highly thought of now than they were when I was a young commis. Those who do not display them in healthy doses, whether they are in a position of responsibility or not, are quickly sidelined. This business takes few prisoners: when the enemy can come from within or from any side at any time there is little time for them.

The fact that everyone has their own opinion is relatively easy to deal with; you just have to know that, at the end of the day, you are still the boss – and that when the boss is right, he is right, and when he is wrong he is right too! But there is another problem that is not so easy to dismiss: when new members of staff arrive from five-star hotels you think they are going to be amazing, but this is not necessarily true. Everywhere, you see, describes a member of staff in a different way. A head waiter at an award-winning restaurant might be described as a manager at another establishment; or a head waiter at one restaurant might be called a waiter somewhere else. These descriptions are not consistent and you are not always able to compare like with like, and therefore your expectations can, on occasion, be completely wrong.

People in this business have become obsessed with titles and business cards. They don't want to be called 'restaurant manager' anymore. They want to be called 'restaurant director' as, in their eyes, a director is more senior. The 'restaurant manager' is running the floor, serving tables and taking orders. But a 'director' suggests someone with far more gravitas: he wears an expensive suit, when he arrives in the mornings he greets the staff, puts his nose in the air, lingers in his office, picks up his umbrella and hat and goes home.

Some sommeliers prefer to be called 'wine buyers'. Again it is all about perception – we do not imagine that a wine buyer would clean the glasses and pour the wine. Instead his responsibility is to buy the wine rather than to serve it. Some people want that impressive title more than anything – a desperate need for the business card.

Many restaurants have succumbed to this, making the restaurant manager the 'restaurant director' and calling the sommelier a 'wine buyer'. These are just glorified titles for people who are doing exactly the same as restaurant managers and sommeliers. These people are busy living their own lie, when they should be concentrating on what matters – progressing and learning.

This serious issue is rooted in the staff and skills shortage the industry is currently facing (we will need more than 700,000 more people in our industry by 2022) and the race to the top from a new generation of professionals. By and large, restaurant owners, chefs and managers across the board have felt they have had no choice but to give in to the pressure and employ more and more directors and executive head chefs, when a few years ago these staff would have merely been head waiters or sous chefs/head chefs. As the vicious circle continues, all we old guard can do is learn how to deal with these new guerrilla tactics.

As the potential new boss of a 'restaurant director', you might look at the title and the business card and employ them in a suitable position, with some leadership duties and responsibilities. Their title implies that they have the right pedigree and so you expect them to be able to run a station and give them the responsibility of welcoming guests, taking an order, making sure the guests' requirements are met – that guests are not given peanuts if they are allergic to peanuts, for instance. But they cannot do it. They cannot run a station, cannot take an order, and they recommend dishes containing nuts to the guest with the dreaded nut allergy. This is because their old job title didn't reflect what they actually did: they weren't ready, but more than anything, they weren't willing.

I remember this guy who came in for an interview, fresh from a very well-known five-star hotel on Park Lane in London. He was a good-looking boy, articulate and eloquent and, as I would discover, he was exceptionally good at customer service – he treated guests well. During the interview he had said all the right things. What were his ambitions? 'I want to be the next general manager. I want to be the next you.' I liked everything he said.

We started him on an induction period, during which he learned the ropes before being moved onto 'the floor' – the dining room – to become a chef de rang running a station. But when it came to it, despite his ambition and his talent for customer service, he could not run the station. He lacked 'the magic touch' – that invisible care that epitomises true hospitality. Good customer service is not enough when you move up to being a chef de rang, because you have to focus on more than one table at once. Your eyes have to be everywhere. His were not. If guests' wine glasses were empty, he missed the fact and had to be summoned to top them up. He served fish to the lady when it was supposed to be for the gentleman. He was not concentrating. I said, 'Look, you obviously have a good pedigree. You are working well but you cannot run the station.'

He replied, 'Okay, but I am just getting used to it.' I told him I was watching him and that he would have to shape up, but the days passed and then the weeks, and he was still not getting any better. Yet he continued to say that that he wanted to be the next me.

When it was time to sit down with him one more time, I said, 'You are very kind to say you want to be the next me, but you can't be the next me if you continue to work like this. It's just not possible. How can you have this ambition and yet perform the way you do? If you want to be the next me you have to be the best waiter.' I must say that the hardest thing to do when dealing with staff is to let them go, because when you let them go, that's it. He had been with us for three months, and I had given him a good run, been patient. So with deep regret, I said, 'I don't think this is going to work. I don't think you really want it. I think there's something on your mind. I can't see what it is.'

Then he admitted it. 'This job is too much for me. I didn't know about the hours.' And then he left.

He did have pedigree and perhaps he could have been superb, but in a different environment. The problem with this world is that until you put someone on the floor and watch them, you will never know how good they are. They could come from the best restaurant in the world, or could come from that little café round the corner, and the one from the little café could turn out to be better. But one thing is certain – you need people. You cannot run a proper establishment alone. So I follow a principle taught to me by my old boss Silvano at Le Gavroche: it is always better to have bad staff than no staff. Even if you have someone who is not particularly good overall, he or she will always be good at something, and that will help you in some way.

At least this particular former employee admitted he was not up to the job, even if it took a while. It is worse when staff that are not very good believe themselves to be excellent, and no amount of pointing this out to them is ever acknowledged. We once had a bar manager, Mark, who was absolutely not up to scratch but he did not realise it. So the rest of us had to work around him, plan for his failings and mistakes, to make sure that the guests never noticed them.

Eventually, I said, 'Mark, you have to understand that I protect you so much, that you are like a little bird inside a nest of cotton wool and I am putting the cotton wool around you to protect you. But really, if I remove all the cotton wool, you are not able to fly and will fall straight to the ground.'

To spell it out I added, 'If you go somewhere else there will be no cotton wool. So really you should be grateful for this cotton wool and work to remove it yourself so you can progress. But at the moment you are being protected and cannot see it. You do not see how lucky you are.' When Mark flapped his wings and eventually left inevitably he fell to earth with a bump.

Many places find themselves having to follow the same maxim as me: better bad staff, than no staff. But this creates a cycle: they protect the bad staff by wrapping them in cotton wool, but when the staff leave the nest and try to fly in your direction then, yes, it is true that they have worked at a nice place and have an impressive title and embossed business cards, but it can turn out that they are completely useless.

It is not just the hierarchy that is changing in restaurants: nowadays increasing numbers of chefs, as well as some maître d's, are opening their own restaurants. This was virtually unheard of 30 years ago, when chefs and front-of-house staff were mere employees.

To the outside world, it might seem easier to run a restaurant if you are a chef, but this is often not the case. They can cook but, of course, it is not just about cooking a steak. Often chefs can't talk to or relate to people; they don't understand how to provide hospitality and how to make guests feel special; they might think it is just about the food, but fail to grasp what this is really about – business and making a healthy profit.

Essential skills and the services that support the business, such as marketing, human resources and/or finance, can be lost on them. But because somebody is willing to back them – or because of the rise of the 'celebrity chef' – they have an inflated sense of their own worth, and this can prove detrimental. Equally, there are maître d's who open their own restaurants, but they don't always understand the kitchen, which is the heart of the business. Without food you don't have a restaurant. You can't just survive on smiles and kindness or, as my mother would say, 'On love and fresh water'. You must have a product to sell and be able to manage the business.

In the best restaurants, people acknowledge their own strengths and appreciate those of others, and the chef and maître d' meet right in the middle.

3

—◄≣

SEE, SMILE AND SAY HELLO

I learned my first lesson in hospitality – one that I have never forgotten – when I was a little boy. I was four or perhaps five years old, and living in Limoges, a historic city in the centre of France that is known throughout the world for its distinctive porcelain.

My brother Pierre and I had been watching cartoons, while our father prepared to go to work. He was a nurse in the hospital, just a few hundred metres from our home. I left my cosy spot in front of the TV and wandered into the bathroom. Dad was shaving in front of the mirror; the father's ritual that fascinates every young child. 'Dad, why do you always shave before you go to work?' I asked.

'Fred, I need to shave,' he said, 'because I need to look the part. If I don't look the part, the patients are not going to trust me.' As he spoke, he continued with the razor, gliding it carefully around his exquisitely clipped moustache. 'They're going to think that I'm a dirty guy. I need to inspire confidence, I need to make sure that they believe in me and that they know that I'm the man who's going to look after them.'

'My appearance says a lot. In a brief way, it tells a long story and a great deal about me.' And of the first impression, he added, 'C'est très, très important, mon petit.' Of course, he was talking about his job as a nurse, but his words stayed with me, and years later I would apply the same exactitude in service.

In the late 1970s there were many elderly people in Limoges who had rarely left the surrounding villages in which they lived. To leave your farm meant to step out of your comfort zone. People spoke not the French that you might understand, but local patois. Finding yourself in the intensive care unit of hospital was a traumatic experience for these people: hooked up to monitors, wires and tubes, feeling completely out of their depth because their farm, their village – their world – was an impossible journey away. Every day of his life my father saw other people's fear of death. One day an old man was brought to hospital; he lay in bed with the sheets up to his eyes; eyes that said he was petrified. My father walked into the room and, in the local patois, said, 'How are you granddad?' Now, from the patient's perspective, here was a man who looked good – handsome, immaculately dressed and, of course, he was clean-shaven, except for his meticulous moustache. My father was a nurse and yet he looked like a doctor. 'How are you granddad?' And the patient's eyes lit up. His fear evaporated, he started to smile and pulled the sheets down from his face.

A connection had been made. Through his appearance and his manner, my father put this anxious man at ease. He showed hospitality, and it worked exactly as it should.

Let's look at that word, hospitality. The ancient Romans used the word *hospitalis*. From this Latin origin, we have the word hospital, hospitable and host. What I do in a restaurant is not about service, but about hospitality. It is about the connection, the bond that can be created in an instant between strangers. Hospitality focuses on how you make people feel and it is accomplished when you make them feel special.

Once his appearance and manner had made his patients feel at ease my father had another trick up his sleeve – he could always make them smile. What was the big trick? Simple! He smiled first.

This was the second lesson in hospitality that I observed in a hospital ward rather than a restaurant. I tell all my staff on reception, 'There is only one thing that you must get right, first and foremost. When people come in to the restaurant, you must see, smile and say hello before they do the same to you.' If you cannot do that then you have failed. It is our job to smile and to be charming first.

The three Ss: see, smile and say hello.

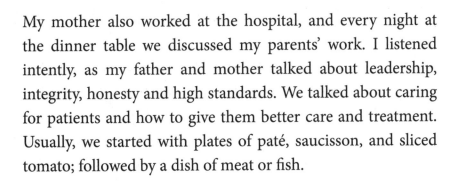

My mother also worked at the hospital, and every night at the dinner table we discussed my parents' work. I listened intently, as my father and mother talked about leadership, integrity, honesty and high standards. We talked about caring for patients and how to give them better care and treatment. Usually, we started with plates of paté, saucisson, and sliced tomato; followed by a dish of meat or fish.

Favourites for dinner chez Sirieix included Lapin à la Moutarde (rabbit braised in a mustard sauce), Boeuf Bourguignon and roast pork with roast potatoes. From time to time Dad (who in summertime was king of the barbecue) made special dishes such as a whole carp, which he stuffed with herbs, garlic and onion.

Cheese came before dessert, as is the French way, and that dessert might have been yoghurt or one of those sweet dishes which epitomise classic French cooking; apple tart, chocolate tart, Crème Brûlée or Crème Caramel. Occasionally, there was a treat from the bakery, be it Eclairs au Chocolat or Roulé au Chocolat; the kind of things you tend not to make home because they are too much work and, anyway, the bakery makes the best.

———

All of this was about nursing and eating as a family and not restaurants, and yet my father saw his patients as guests, and it was his personal mission to give them his best. So, from an early age I understood the basis of customer service. Those dinner-table chats and delicious food left me with an appreciation for high values and professionalism, as well as the necessity to have pride in your appearance. Leadership, I realised and learned through my father, is about what you do, not what you say. He was irritated by others who did not work with the same commitment: five out of ten was not good enough, it had to be ten out of ten.

The hospital was like a second home for me, and I was often there, seeing my mother or father. Their colleagues and patients were pleased when I tottered in – 'Oh little Fred!' – and they always made a fuss of me. 'He's so adorable and sweet … So funny …' I felt like the king of the castle, making them laugh and telling them stories. To me, this was my parents' hospital – they owned the place, it seemed to me – and I felt completely at ease and happy when I was there.

There was one room that fascinated my young mind. It was filled with computers that monitored the medical equipment in the Intensive Care Unit. My dad said, 'You see, this is technology. We are very good with technology … We are at the forefront of what we do. We are one of the leading hospitals in the world.'

He viewed himself, rightly, as part of a large team. His qualities as a nurse improved the service, but the service was the sum of all the parts. My father was giving me the greatest education I would need for my profession in later life: the principles of patient care in hospitals are similar to those for customer care in hospitality or, indeed, any business.

I recall, for instance, my father telling my mother about his conversation with another employee who had cleaned a room. 'Well, I walked into the room and it was filthy. I said to her, "Please tell me, you believe you have cleaned this room, but would you put your mother in there?" She went straight back into that room and cleaned it again. It was spotless.' Of course, this high regard for hygiene and cleanliness is also the bedrock of the hospitality business. Whether you are a nurse, a waiter or a chef, if you are sloppy, then it is fair to say you do not care one single jot about your work.

Now, think of the waiter. Already, we've learned that he does not require much in order to do the job well. He must be clean, smell clean, look clean, and be impeccable at all times. Well-polished shoes and a decent memory are essential. As the waiter, you have to be focused and be ready for action – have your wits about you. You must maintain high standards and have zero tolerance for a laissez-faire attitude and negligence.

Then there is the smile. The smile is an integral part of the uniform. No one would think or dare to come to work without their shirt or trousers, so don't you dare come to work for me without your smile. No matter what is happening in your life, in service you must keep on smiling and you need to want to make people happy. That is all you have, and you need nothing more. You do not need to tell me, your boss, that you are good. If you are good, I will see it, don't worry about that. Just do your job, smile, have fun and enjoy. There are no problems in life or in service – just solutions. Be the best. Be dedicated, hospitable and smile because you are proud to be in the business we call hospitality.

So, if it is that simple, how do people stand out? Well, I think that service is like the production line of a car factory, but with one crucial difference. With both, you know exactly what you need to do. In a factory, at one end you have the raw materials and, as the parts come down the conveyor belt, the production line puts them together to make the car. No matter what country a factory making a particular brand of car happens to be in – Britain, France, China, America or Japan – you still end up with each car being identical.

Service is similar. You know what you need to do: look after your guests. In a way, the customer journey in a restaurant is like the conveyor belt of a factory. But here is the crucial difference. In the factory, the conveyor belt has only one side to it; it is a mechanical, robotic process. This is the 'what'. In service, there are two sides. You not only have the 'what', crucially, you also have the 'how' you achieve it. This is the hardest part to get right because it is about perception; the customer's perception.

The best way to do this is to establish distinct touchpoints in every customer journey. By creating touchpoints you can help every waiter, even the bad ones, to get to the right result – or at least you can try. Every single touchpoint is there for a specific purpose and must be able to create trust. In religion trust is the basis of love. In business trust is the basis of loyalty. And loyalty cannot exist without reliability and consistency, hence why it is so vital to have a well-defined customer journey. For example, meeting and greeting customers at reception is both the most basic and the mother of all standards. The basic is just *what* you do, because every restaurant is supposed to do it. The key to a great restaurant is *how* you do it. For me, it is all about the three Ss – see, smile and say hello. This is the first of the touchpoints in any restaurant I run. It is non-negotiable, and if you don't get it, then you are out.

A customer journey can have 15, 20, 25 or more touch points depending on the establishment or business, and any business that deals with customers has or should have such a journey mapped out purposefully and distinctively. It is the only way to deliver a consistently high experience to customers, so you must ensure that all staff know what they have to do and how they should do it.

4

LEARNING THE ROPES

Thanks to my parents, even as a child I had a keen sense of hospitality, and not just through their work at the hospital. Despite working night shifts, building our house and coaching the local football team during the day, my parents still found the time for fun and hosted countless dinner parties. We always had somebody at home to join us at the table, whether it was friends or family. My mother might cook for ten or 20 people and would serve fried fillet steak, sautéed lamb sweetbreads, or huge fish pies baked in the oven. It was like going to a restaurant, and everyone was welcome. Our door was always open.

Food features heavily in my earliest memories. I remember Christmas at my grandmother's, when I was about three or four, and eating snails and frog's legs with lots of wine. There was warmth and love, which was ultimately reassuring to me, as it would be to any child. I felt so secure and loved. 'Oh, Freddie's so funny … Fred, can you sing? … Fred, can you tell a story?' Throughout my childhood I was called upon to be funny, sing and tell stories.

My parents' approach to life has carried me through my own – a life in service. They tried hard to please others, and were constantly thinking of how others would benefit from their actions. Wouldn't it be wonderful if this attitude was more common?

In fact, my father used to get lots of tips from patients. This was unusual and it was probably not allowed. Nevertheless, patients would press a few notes into his hand as they left the hospital. He did not keep the money for himself, as you might imagine. Instead, the cash went into a box, and would eventually help pay for a meal when he and the staff went to a restaurant for an outing.

As staunch defenders of hospital 'service', they would go on strike when necessary. Dad had played a role in the union but, following a big argument, he told them – right in the middle of *l'assemblée générale* (the regular union meeting) – that he had had enough, that they could 'go stuff themselves' and he then resigned. During one demonstration in Paris, things turned sour. My father and his colleagues found themselves face to face with the CRS, the feared riot police, who were in helmets and wielding batons. In the midst of the action, my father saw a young policeman, who was about 20 years old, and tapped on his helmet. The policeman looked at my father who, above the roar of the crowd, smiled and jokingly said, 'Does your mother know what you're doing here?' The cop smiled too. My dad can make friends and reach out and connect with anyone in any circumstances.

Contrast that with the time my mother went on strike in Limoges. Afterwards, I asked how it went and she said, 'Well, we demonstrated for a bit … And then we went for a meal at a lovely restaurant and had a wonderful time!'

No matter what the circumstances, food and having a good time were always a family priority. I believe the fact that I was raised with a very strong sense of how important these things are is what has shaped my career, but I can only see that now when I look back. When I first thought about the idea of a career in restaurants, I was determined to be a chef, with no desire whatsoever to work front of house.

I was certainly not a model pupil at school. When I think of *l'école primaire* (primary school), the first memory that pops into my mind is this: befriending a boy who had cigarettes aged ten. Or rather, befriending a boy because he had cigarettes. He was kind enough to let me have a puff or two, and then a teacher caught us. My mother was informed. 'I did not do it,' I lied to her. 'Freddie's in trouble again,' she said to my father when he returned from work. 'He's got no limits. He doesn't know when to stop being naughty.' No limits were a problem for my mother, but in the restaurant world having no limits is an asset – you don't stop until the job is done and you see ways to solve problems that others don't.

My *lycée* (secondary school) was so huge it felt impersonal. I spent my days missing the closeness of home life, and wandered the long corridors thinking, 'What the hell am I doing here?'

Hope came one day during a bus journey, when I shared a seat with an older friend who was no longer a student and had a job. 'What do you do?' I asked.

'I'm an apprentice pastry chef.'

'Ahh. Tell me about the job. What does it involve?'

'I bake bread and I make pastries.'

'When do you work?'

'I start at 3 o'clock in the morning, and finish at about noon.' he said.

He gave me a hearty 'au revoir' as we reached his stop, and I was left on the bus thinking, 'Well, that sounds good, I want to be a pastry chef.' It was serendipity. What appealed to me was the idea that, should I become a baker, I would be different to other people (except for my friend on the bus) as I would work unusual hours. No limits!

At home, I said to my mother, 'I have decided that I am going to be a pastry chef.'

'What?'

'Yeah.'

'Freddie, that's crazy,' said my mother. But once she had given it some thought, she added, 'You're better off being a chef, rather than specialising in patisserie. If you are a chef you can cook more things so will have more options.'

'Ahh, okay,' I said. 'That sounds like a good idea.' So in a matter of seconds, I had switched from a specialist job to a broader role in the kitchen. As a chef, I would also be able to learn about patisserie and bread. The naïveté of youth!

The next stage was to apply to catering college. I filled in the application form for the Lycée Hôteliers de Souillac, in the medieval town of Souillac, close to the Dordogne river. When I say that I applied, it was actually my mother who meticulously researched France's catering colleges, and she chose this particular one – it was ranked number three in France. Souillac is in the Lot region of south-west France, about 130km from my home in Limoges, and if I was successful, it would be like going to boarding school. This college was so highly regarded that they only accepted one-tenth of applicants. So we also applied to other schools too, just in case.

I was offered a place at a college in Limoges, which was okay, but I had really been hoping for Souillac, which of course was more prestigious. Then, a week before the school term was due to start, I got a call from the lycée in Souillac offering me a place. In my bedroom, I packed my bags as the radio played Yazz singing 'The Only Way is Up'. It was September 1988, and I was off to spend the next four years at the Lycée Hôteliers de Souillac.

Arriving in the medieval town, with its ancient abbey and cobbled streets, I did not have a clue what to expect, I just knew I wanted to be a chef. I had no idea that I was about to meet two extraordinary men who would have a profound influence on my life.

The first was Robert Canton who, since 1976, had been the headmaster, or *le proviseur*. Canton did not follow conventional teaching methods. He was a maverick. This instantly appealed to me because he ran the college as if it was a private business. His focus was on quality, by which I mean the quality of the young men and women who were under his care and tutelage. He thought of the future – how to shape his students for life – as well as the present. His primary concern was not only that his students would find a job when they qualified, but that they would never be out of work. In this quest he was phenomenally successful. When the students left Canton's catering college, they walked straight into jobs, usually good ones. There must be thousands of them now working in the top places all over the world.

Canton invested a great deal in the quality of the teaching. Discipline was of a military standard – good training for the world we were going into. Every morning we were lined up like soldiers, and there was a roll call. Sometimes, as we stood upright and to attention, Canton would come and address us. He was as tall as he was large, with a great physical presence. He had little hair, a big stomach and was not dissimilar in appearance to Alfred Hitchcock. 'Students!' he would bellow, and his young audience immediately quietened down to listen to his every word.

One day we had a pillow fight in the dormitory and the older students, who were aged about 19 or 20 and were meant to be in charge of us, were unable to stop the commotion. Suddenly, the long shadow of Proviseur Canton fell across the floor. Most of us were able to hide, but one of the students received a mighty backhander (or two) from Canton. Such was the common 'teaching technique' in those days. His occasional lapses of temper, however, did nothing to alter the admiration that we had for him as a leader. Once I had settled in, which did not take long, I felt firmly as if I was on the right course in life. Unlike my earlier experiences of school, here I was one of the best students.

In general I was serious and studious; my homework was always handed in on time, and mostly I was top of the class. We spent that first year studying service and cookery, both of which I did well in. I learned to make the French classics; Coq au Vin, Veau Marengo, Boeuf Bourguignon, Salade Niçoise, Sole Meunière, Soupe de Poisson, Crème Pâtissière, Béchamel sauce and so on. During the first two years, I made weekly trips home, taking a train to Limoges every Saturday morning. As I walked through the front door, my mother would tell me to do my homework. It seemed as if I only had a few hours of free time before taking the train back to Souillac on Sunday afternoon. A few weeks before my placement, I made the customary weekend trip to Limoges to visit my parents. By the end of that weekend, I would have changed my career path, and all because of some pasta.

I had the recipe for pasta, and was confident I could make it, but I underestimated the amount my recipe would give me. I ended up with sheets of the stuff and, as I started to cut millions of strands of tagliatelle and hang them up to dry in the kitchen, I soon ran out of space. Every cupboard door and chair was covered with long strips of pasta. I gave some to our neighbours' dog but that still left masses. My father came into the kitchen, and stood silent, shocked almost by the sight of what I had created. Then he said, 'Fred, you want to be a chef. Are you sure?' It was at that second that something clicked inside me. He was right. I thought to myself, 'I can't be a chef.' Although I could cook, I could also see that life as a chef was not for me, partly because I did not want to spend my time following recipes, which meant that this sort of thing would definitely happen again, and also because I did not want to be shut away in a kitchen. Many chefs will tell you of the sense of freedom they get from being in a kitchen but I was not that person. For me, the freedom existed in the dining room. I had always loved watching my parents at the hospital, making people happy and that was really why I had gone to catering college, to learn how to do the same thing in a restaurant. Over very big plates of pasta that night, I said to my parents, 'I can change my option at college, and that's what I'm going to do. I'm not going to be a chef. I am going to be a waiter.'

—◄≣

I returned to Canton's lycée in Souillac, but from that point on I would be training in the Service department. Here, I was extremely fortunate to be taught by Alain Sourzac, the second man at Souillac to have a tremendous influence on my life.

He truly knew everything there was to know about service. For that reason we referred to him as God. 'I can't meet you for lunch – I have a lesson with God.' With reddish-blond hair, a beard and the warmest smile known to mankind, he was like a big, friendly teddy bear. He was 40 years old, although to me, in my late teens, he looked older. I know he was 40 because one day I asked, 'How old are you, Monsieur Sourzac.'

'I'm 40.'

'Seulement?' I said. Only?

God raised an eyebrow. 'Fred,' he said, 'You have missed an opportunity to shut up.'

Other students giggled, but later when I reflected on what he had said, I realised that God had taught me another important lesson about service (and life, in general). You have to be careful what you say and when you say it. You must be sensitive. This goes against my spontaneous nature, and Sourzac was the first person to show me how to manage it.

God was an absolute master of the profession, and one to observe and revere. If he was standing in the middle of a busy dining room, he seemed to know what every single member of his waiting staff were doing, even if they seemed to be hidden away in the corner of the room. We all worked hard for him, constantly craving his admiration and praise, hoping for a smile and a 'Bravo!' There were other teachers, but everybody considered God to be the best, and that's because he was the best.

With his firm moral stance, he was not dissimilar to my father; straight as a die and never two-faced. He did not drink to excess, like a few other teachers I could name but won't. He did not flirt with the girls, like a few other teachers I could name but won't. He was forever inspiring and would instil in us the importance of working, and of continuing to work at all costs, once we had left college. He was insistent that we should go on to work not just in any old restaurant, but in five-star hotels or restaurants of great repute. Quality places. 'Don't go and work with the riff-raff in, say, the little Pizzeria da Mario, or Brasserie du Marché. Avoid the mediocre. Go to the top restaurants.'

This advice was always in my mind, and I became determined to aim for the top. There is a French proverb, which God delivered daily and with dramatic effect: 'Qui peut le plus, peut le moins.' He who can do the most, can do the least. Who can argue with this saying? If you can work first in the finest establishment, then afterwards it will be easy to work anywhere.

God thrived on the creation of excellence. As with Monsieur Canton, he strived for quality, in terms of work, but also from a moral standpoint. We should be good people, he said, and I have tried to maintain this principle.

For the first couple of years, I shared a room with a fellow student. While most students revised before lights-out, we would host parties that went on until one or two o'clock in the morning. With about a dozen friends crammed into our little room, we drank wine, and ate all sorts of cheese, saucisson and ham. We even found a clever method of heating cassoulet – the casserole of beans, sausage and duck or goose legs. We put an element in boiling water and then into the big pot of cassoulet. Delicious! We had to be up at seven the next morning for roll call, but we had the energy of youth on our side even though we were often exhausted. On Wednesdays, we had afternoons free, so would go to the Dordogne with our girlfriends.

The waiting staff did not always mix with the chefs. This suited me fine because the school's bullies seemed to be the students who were learning to become chefs and not waiters. One of the aspiring chefs was about twice my size and we got into a disagreement as we were walking into class. I do not remember who started the argument, but he finished it by giving me a dead leg. Oh the pain! I could barely walk and soon I had a massive bruise on my right thigh. Back at home, my father applied one of those big plasters that releases heat, and wrapped it in bandages. I must have left it on for too long, and rather than healing the bruise, layers of skin were removed. I lost the bruise but gained a scab. We were all heading off for a school skiing trip and, as I could hardly walk, I definitely could not ski. I said to the bully, 'If you ever do that again, I'm not going to Monsieur Canton. I'm going to the police.' His rock-hard kneecap never met my thigh again.

———◄

My weekend trips home became a little more infrequent, as I sometimes found a way of earning money by waiting in the restaurants of Souillac. For this I was paid about 400 French francs, cash in hand and therefore tax free. This was a sizeable income, and the money was usually spent on nice shoes and, on one occasion, a leather jacket. Aside from the money, I enjoyed the work. There was more of it on Saturdays, when I started waiting on tables at weddings. As part of the school curriculum, I also worked in the Restaurant d'Application within the lycée, where anyone could come and eat the food that was cooked and served by the student chefs and waiters. It was like a workshop where we would gain experience, and we were not paid.

Life took an interesting turn when I put myself up for President of the Student Federation, and won the election. This propelled me into a working relationship of sorts with Robert Canton. To other students he was a formidable character, so much so that they would turn ashen-faced and almost faint at the prospect of entering his office. But he did not scare me one bit; he was just like any other man. I found him compelling and enjoyable to be with. I would sit on the other side of his desk, happily listening to his wise words about the industry and his plans for the college. I must have inherited from my father the ability to converse, connect and engage with anyone, from the cleaner to the VIP or police, and Canton was indeed a Very Important Person (or a *Très Important*, as I like to call them).

Students tend to be left wing politically, and in France they are not really students until they have been on a strike or two, as is the nation's culture. I had been raised on strikes, with my parents cheerfully joining picket lines at any given opportunity. In my role as president, I was in a position not only to go on strikes and demonstrations, but to organise them. And that is what I did.

When I heard of a huge demonstration taking place in Toulouse, I wasted no time in arranging for us to be present. This was the chance for a fantastic jolly for my friends and me. First, it meant that we would miss college. Second, we would be able to relish an adventure, drink a bit, perhaps, and then a bit more. And perhaps we would meet some girls there, and eat bowls of cassoulet – the dish that Toulouse claims as its own. Obviously, as poor students, we did not have much cash for travelling. So we would have to find an entrepreneurial way to reach the demo, the drink, the girls and the cassoulet.

I telephoned Souillac train station. 'Hello, my fellow students and I will be attending a demonstration in Toulouse. I wondered if you would be kind enough to let us travel on the train for free.'

'For free?'

'Yes, for free. For nothing.'

'How many of you will be going?'

'About 300.'

'300?'

'Yes, there will be about 300 of us.'

He asked me to hold, and when he came back on the line

he said, 'That shouldn't be a problem.' I told you, strikes are an essential part of French culture.

So 300 students put aside catering, cooking, hospitality and service, and boarded the train from Souillac to Toulouse. Never has an SNCF train reeked more of spilt beer and cannabis fumes. About two hours later, when we poured ourselves into Toulouse, we demonstrated in the streets and avenues of what the French know as *La Ville Rose* (after its pink city walls). We were on a mission to paint the pink town red. I have little recollection of the rest of the trip, and cannot remember what the strike was about.

Struck down with strike fever, I organised another event. This time it was a sit-down protest. About 100 of us marched from the catering school to the outskirts of Souillac, and then sat down in the middle of the A20. At that time it was the only main road between Toulouse and Paris so it was pretty busy. Or rather, it was usually pretty busy, but on that particular Friday afternoon on either side of us, there were two almighty tailbacks of Citroëns and Renaults. We sat there for four hours, surrounded by a regiment of police officers, serenaded by a thousand honking car horns. We were singing about freedom and saying no to reforms for education, though precisely what the reforms were I cannot remember.

Afterwards, I was not entirely proud of the sit-in, or sit-down. We had prevented thousands of law-abiding citizens from returning to their homes and seeing their families after a gruelling day at work.

Those were my striking days. Now I am all for employees' rights but I don't believe strikes are the solution. The French have been brought up on them – they do not know any better.

My crusading extra-curricular activities increased one day – or one evening, over cassoulet and red wine in my room – when I had a brainwave: I would launch a student newspaper. Impassioned, I went to see Monsieur Canton to share my brilliant idea. He listened with patience. Then he asked, 'So Fred, who will be in this newspaper? Who will write for it?'

I told him I would write this bit and that bit – oh, and probably another bit – and then four of my friends would contribute the other pieces.

Gently, Monsieur Canton said, 'Hmm. Five of you. I just want to tell you something. This is your newspaper and you and your four friends will write the first issue. I like it, it's nice, but what are you going to do about the second issue?' I did not have an immediate response, it must be said. He continued, 'Sometimes these newspapers are put together by a small circle of friends. But then it runs out of steam and the project dies because people don't have the time to commit to it.' In the most diplomatic and thoughtful way he was trying to tell me my plan would never work as it was just me and a handful of friends.

After his spiel, I said, 'Oh, don't worry. It'll be fine.'

We produced one issue. There was never a second one. Proviseur Canton was correct, as ever. I had already been aware of the importance of teamwork, but this venture reinforced my view. Collaboration and partnership are crucial. You can have an idea or a vision, but a leader is skilled when he or she brings others on board, surrounding himself with people who understand and appreciate the vision. The result is longevity, something my newspaper did not have.

At the end of every term there was a highlight in the form of an invitation to the Sourzac's home, and over wine, ham and cheese, we would ogle God's wife: Madame Sourzac was a beautiful woman. As we chatted and drank wine, our teacher would update us on the progress of his book, a tome about etiquette. He was certainly the perfect man to write about the subject, although I am not sure his manuscript was ever published. He would smile that wonderful smile, and say to us, 'Do you know what? The day I stop being a teacher I will open a job agency. And I will find the best jobs for all of my students.'

That did not happen. In the summer of 2009 many of Monsieur Sourzac's protégés received a phone call from his daughter. It was terribly sad news. 'I am sorry to say that Papa has passed away. Cancer.' she said. 'But he felt there were people who should know and so he left a list of those we should phone … And that is why I am calling …' That was Alain Sourzac. As faultlessly detailed and considerate in his final days, as he was throughout his life. How fitting that in his honour, an award of excellence was created. I will always remember the teachings of Monsieur Sourzac and Monsieur Canton. They added much-needed rigour to my initial instincts and education at my parents' knees, and provided me with the foundations of everything I have built today.

Though Sourzac and Monsieur Canton taught me everything I know, the place that made me fall in love with this profession was a restaurant I worked in during one summer of my time at college. It was not a fancy restaurant; not a sombre temple of gastronomy with tasting menus and a weighty bible of expensive wines. Instead, it was a cheap and very cheerful place in the medieval town of Sarlat, in the beautiful Dordogne.

The restaurant's name, Le Bon Chabrol, says it all. In the south-west of France, they like to pour a splash of wine into their soup before bringing the bowl to the lips and slurping it down. This custom is known as *faire chabrol*. So, loosely translated, the restaurant was called 'The Good Slurp'. It was nothing grand: a fun and friendly neighbourhood restaurant, but often these establishments can be the best of them all, can't they?

Tourists – and there were always plenty of them in town – came to enjoy the region's specialties and wines. There were duck dishes of Cassoulet, Magret de Canard and Confit Canard. We served foie gras, of course, and Pommes Salardaise, that comforting dish of potatoes, sliced and baked in goose fat and heaps of garlic. The boss made the best use of me, and I was thrown to the lions from the word go. There were no job titles in this restaurant. No such thing as head waiter or manager. Just the boss, his wife and the staff (kitchen and front of house).

I would welcome the guests – 'Bonjour Madame, Monsieur' – take them to their table and seat them, take their aperitif order, make their aperitif, take their wine order, take their food order, serve the food and wine, clear the table, give them the bill, and then re-set the table. Basically, as a waiter, here you did it all. The restaurant had 150 covers and some days I looked after the whole terrace alone – 50 covers! The pace was fast. Dash, dash, dash.

I loved it. I just got on with the job, morning to late at night, thriving on adrenaline. As the bells of the ancient cathedral rang out during the day and the sun shone gloriously, I felt at home. And – please forgive my pride, I say this in all humility – I realised I was good at the job; very good, in fact, which was a confidence-booster like nothing I had previously known. At about midnight – after wishing 'bonne nuit' to the departing stragglers – and then locking up, I would head back to my digs. When my housemates asked how the day had gone, they did not get an 'Oh, it was fine,' or, 'Not bad.' Instead I would talk with passion and great interest about the service and how it went. I could remember every single dish or wine ordered by any of the guests, the mood at each table and the interaction with my colleagues. It was a special time. An awakening!

Head on pillow, I would replay the day in my mind, as if I were watching a magical movie. Then I would drift off to sleep for a few hours, before waking up, leaping out of bed – shower, dress and a quick café – before rushing back to Le Bon Chabrol in rue des Armes, and beginning all over again. My smile never vanished. The restaurant, however, did. It is no longer there and, since the early 1990s, I have been mostly in Britain and in London. Yet the memories have not faded, and the joy of giving, sharing and looking after people has only grown within me. You see, service is like a religion. It is a way to engage and connect with guests, colleagues and the suppliers of food and wine. It is my life.

5

———◀≡

THE ART OF WAR

As you've already seen, service can be pressed into many metaphors. I can't help it! I'm French. But there's one I come back to more than any other. The battle; the long war, and the strategies you need to succeed.

As a student, I was fascinated by history and, in particular, military history. Perhaps there was an emphasis on the subject because of the place where I grew up. Over the centuries, the people of Limoges had a reputation for fighting the aggressor. This is a region of France where battles have been won and lost. During the One Hundred Years War, the town was under French control before it was seized by the English led by Edward, the Black Prince. During the Second World War, it was a focus point for the French Resistance. There were figures that I felt very passionately about – particularly Georges Guinguoin, a celebrated French resistance fighter during the Second World

War, who started the fight for France in Limoges and took it to the forests around the city. I carried their example with me through my early career. But it was really a book called *The Art of War*, which I read in my mid-twenties, that has shaped my approach to service and convinced me that the key to success in service is exactly the same as it is for war.

Written by Sun Tzu, a great Chinese general of the 5th century BC, the book covers each and every nuance of battle. It was given almost biblical status by the warlords of ancient China, and when it was translated by the Europeans in the 18th century, its influence spread to the west. Napoleon and General McArthur are among many commanders who have drawn inspiration from the pages of *The Art of War*.

The book helped them win wars, perhaps. For me, it remains a guide that can also be applied to service, and how to be the best in this profession. I realise the comparison cannot be a literal one – the only real weapons in the dining room are the steak knives – and of course I do not really regard guests as the enemy, but there are rules of engagement, organisation and preparation in dealing with both, and you also have to be prepared for anything.

Above all else, *The Art of War* concentrates on studying the enemy, knowing where the attack will come from, and choosing when and how to fight. Its content is as tactical as it is philosophical, and when I read it I think, 'Okay, I need to get all the little things right in order to win the battle.' I have read the book many times and whenever I do I seem to learn something new.

Where do you start? With your first line of defence. In a restaurant, the first line of defence is everything that the guests can see, feel, touch and smell before you, the restaurateur, have delivered a single dish to them. Let's start with the outlier, the spy sent to lure people in from enemy lines: your restaurant's website. The site has to be well designed, with beautiful photographs. It should be informative, engaging, and the visitor must be able to find and navigate the site easily. Most importantly, your phone number should be immediately obvious.

Then, when the telephone rings, it must be answered within three rings and in a friendly, welcoming manner – something that must be practised and rehearsed to perfection. Excellence is about what you repeatedly do. As Aristotle said, 'excellence, therefore, is a habit, not an act.'

The caller should have a sense of a smile down the line, and be left feeling, 'Wow, these guys are so professional.' Speed is fundamental – the caller does not have time to waste: make the reservation, be clear about when you will confirm it, and leave them to get on with their day with a smile on their face.

That's the outliers. Now, what about the actual first line? This all begins at reception. Reception is what I call the Japanese Garden. In Japan, the garden focuses on the separation of its elements: wood, stone, earth, water and metals. This creates the effect of looking clean because it is clean. A Japanese garden is not weed-infested, with overgrown shrubs and crumbling brickwork. In the same way, a restaurant's reception must never be messy, strewn with paperwork, pens, mobile phones and other bits and bobs. It has to be tidy, inviting: everything in its place. People go to restaurants for so many reasons, for an experience, or to escape the clutter of life. They don't want to be confronted by more of it. Neatness and cleanliness sends out a subliminal message: it says the staff are focussed and organised, and nothing is distracting them from the job of service.

And, of course, at reception there must be a greeter, who has an abundance of genuine charm and a God-given desire to make people happy. They have to be the embodiment of the three Ss: see, smile and say hello.

I have a nickname for the people on reception at Galvin at Windows. I call them 'the gazelles on Red Bull' and it is meant as a huge compliment. As you are aware, a gazelle is a wild animal that is particularly aware of its surroundings. Even if the gazelle is looking to the east, it can still see or sense the lion approaching from the west, north or south. In order to stay alive, the gazelle must avoid the lion. The people on reception are like gazelles because they are aware; they have an animal sense of what is going on around them. And they are gazelles on Red Bull because they are not just aware, but super-aware. The lion could come at any minute, but they will be ready.

As you know by now, my cardinal rule at reception is that you must see, smile and say hello to people before they see, smile and say hello to you. This is completely non-negotiable.

Hospitality is about giving first and giving generously, making people feel special and engaging and connecting with them. When the guests arrive, they leave their coats and their worries in the cloakroom, and they receive that first smile. Being able to do this naturally is the 'tell' of a truly excellent waiter. It can be taught, of course, but that rare person who has the instinct to do it with no training is very special indeed.

In battle, the commander cannot simply focus on one small part of the action. He needs to have an eye on the whole field. If I am talking to a guest, I need to give him my full and undivided attention. But I must also be aware if somebody else walks into the room and wants or requires my attention. That is the art of good service. But this is hard work! 'Victory belongs,' said Napoleon, 'to the most persevering.' This is as true of hospitality, as in many other aspects of life. In a way, in the restaurant business we persevere to do the same thing every day. Different people come, different meals are served, and yet expectations remain the same. You have to stay fully focused. One way to help this, I have found, is repetition of the obvious. Because by definition nothing is obvious until it becomes obvious. Constant repetition of what one should do in service ensures that it ends up being done. 'I want you to say goodbye … I want you stand here … I want you to do that …' Staff need to know what they are doing, and often they need to be told what do, again and again, until it becomes completely instinctive; until you become a gazelle. Muhammad Ali, a boxer rather than a waiter, of course, put it best of all: 'It is the repetition of affirmation that leads to belief, and once that belief becomes a deep conviction things begin to happen.' Then you just need to find your Red Bull.

So, you're nearly through the first line of defence. But there's one final hurdle: the walk from reception to your table. Every good restaurant will have a plan for this walk. You want to keep your guest happy (as, conversely, in war you want to keep your enemy guessing and completely alert). At Galvin at Windows, we have the Five Smiles, which ensures that the feeling of being welcome and that we are entirely ready for the guest will continue throughout their time at the restaurant.

The first smile is from the gazelle on Red Bull. On the way to the table, the guest will pass or see four more members of the team: the manager, a waiter here, a waiter there, and so on, and maybe another who sees the guest from a distance. With each smile, there might also be a cheerful greeting: 'Hello, how are you?' Five smiles, perhaps in 20 seconds, but all absolutely crucial in making sure the guest feels completely welcomed.

Accompanying the five smiles on the walk is the vista – the view of the dining room itself. There is symmetry to the tables and chairs; they follow a line, they must follow a line, so that the chairs are perfectly situated in front of the tables; not pushed under the table but flush to it. Balance equals beauty: compare my crooked nose to David Gandy's, if you want proof. As the guest walks in, the room should be so perfectly balanced that they cannot think anything other than: 'This has been set up by people who care.'

All this ensures that when the guest sits down, they will already be thinking, 'Everybody is so nice here.' Remember, they are yet to eat or drink. They have only encountered the first line of defence. When they do eat and drink, the guest has been put in such a good mood that the food and the wine will taste better than they otherwise might have done. This process – the creation of harmony in a restaurant – sounds so simple and obvious, but a great deal of thought and hours and hours of training have gone into making it happen and seemingly run smoothly.

What next? The Magic Touch: the waiter pulls out the chair so that the guest can sit down. It is a magic touch because it is nothing really – a courteous act – but at the same time it is everything because it is an art that leaves the guest feeling happy and special. It is simply paying attention to human nature and psychology, being in exactly the right place at the right time. The guest is thinking, 'Wow, the food already tastes fantastic – and I've not eaten a thing!'

But it isn't over yet. (Of course, in a restaurant, it is never over. There is always a threat looming on the horizon and you must defend these touchpoints at all costs.) You see, once seated, the guest still remains at that first line of defence until they have a drink. At this point, and in fact at all times, never – ever – leave a guest alone with his thoughts. This is very important. By this, I do not mean you should never leave the guest alone. Instead, you should never leave a guest to wonder about what might be happening next.

You must anticipate what the guest would like or might ask for. How often have you sat in a restaurant and thought, 'When is my drink coming? When is my food coming? When am I going to order? Who is looking after me? Where are the toilets? Where is my bill?' All of these questions, and more, should not arise. They are questions that will begin the minute the guest is at the table, usually with the thought, 'What shall I have to drink?' Therefore you, as the waiter, must ask the guest what they would like to drink before they have had time to think of it.

At Galvin at Windows, the moment the guest is seated, he or she is given the menu, and two postcards. 'These are for you.' The guest sees the postcards – a little gift. The photos on the cards feature views of London from the restaurant. We are in a beautiful location and it is about showing and demonstrating our values before anything: we will post the cards anywhere in the world with our compliments. Then the service begins, by which point we have not simply told the guest about our values, namely hospitality and generosity, but we have already demonstrated them.

When all of the above is put into practice, within a few moments the guest is confident that he is in the right place and will be looked after extremely well. Just as the triumph of battle depends to a great extent on expert strategy, so too does the success of service. There is a structure and the more stable this structure is, the more quickly we can establish trust, and thus the better the experience for the guest who can absolutely trust us to make sure his experience is a good one.

These standards must not slip. As the guest awaits his drink, he is still at the first line of defence, and now he has time to glance at the table: it is laid with yet more consideration for balance, symmetry and beauty. The cutlery, for example, needs to be set wide enough apart to allow space for the first plate to be placed in front of the guest.

To the eye, the symmetry is pleasing, and helps to create confidence and trust in the experience. But there is also a practical reason for this: when the starter arrives, there is no need for the waiter to move the cutlery. If the cutlery was set in a thoughtless style, there could be chaos when the starter is served: the guest might have to move his chair; the waiter might have to bend slightly, to lean across the table, putting his head in between the guest and his companion. It can get even messier if the dish is hot. We want to avoid all of the potential dangers, risks and hazards. Everything must be in the right place when the guest is seated.

If there seems to be a lot of detail in this chapter, it is because every detail matters. At the beginning of his or her customer journey, the guest might think, 'This is amazing.' But at the end of the experience, the guest will only think it is amazing if every touchpoint – everything you do for the guest – is indeed amazing. Consistency is crucial. Otherwise, you might be taking the guest on a sliding scale, moving from 'amazing' downwards. As the restaurateur, you want to accomplish a nine or ten out of ten from each guest's mental scoreboard. If you achieve lower than nine then the next time he wants to eat out, the guest will go somewhere else, you will be down in business, and that is not a good place to be.

The Art of War also covers the significance of spies. As with battle, an element of spying is crucial in this business. You need to know what your competitors are up to, and you are a fool if you think you don't. What do the competitors think? What do they do? What is on their menus and how good, or bad, is their website? You must look, and be curious. A restaurant cannot exist in isolation. If you are at war you need to know what is going on. Restaurateurs must observe their rivals, and scrutinise the way they run their business. In war, the referee is absent. Each side is desperate to win and there is nothing that they will not do to accomplish victory. In restaurants, a guest choosing to eat at a rival establishment means that you are losing money, and we are all desperate not to.

Spies and spying are vital in this. Good 'intel' can lead to victory. So, you check your competitors' prices, you check their menus, try to find out about their ideas, subscribe to their newsletters, and you talk to people. As Shakespeare wrote, 'Listen to many, speak to a few.' That means that you keep your ear to the ground, you listen to everybody and absorb what they have to say.

Ask questions, no matter how innocent. Ask a waiter, 'Oh, how are you today? Where are you from? Is everything okay? Oh you're busy today – how is business?' Very soon the conversation will be flowing, and little morsels of information emerge. 'Well, we are doing this deal with so-and-so … The average spend is down … Very down …'

'Listening to many' means, essentially, that you can gather nuggets of information that enable you to find out what your rivals are doing and how they do it, and this might enable you to do it better than them. It is all about understanding the competition, which is even more important in London these days, as an increasing number of competitors appear on the restaurant scene.

Things have changed in the quarter of a century since I came to Britain. Today there are so many exceptional restaurants that have not won traditional awards, but they are exceptional nevertheless, and they care about food, service and their guests.

So spies and spying are part of restaurant life. But the poaching of staff is considered to be below the belt – unacceptable. But this is war, and you need to win. So how can you pull it off?

Let's assume I am in a restaurant, and I have just enjoyed a meal and received the most incredible service. A part of me wants to say to the waiter or waitress, 'You are fantastic. Leave your job here. Start work for me tomorrow.' To say such a thing would be a serious breach of restaurant etiquette and must never happen. Instead, the business card is called for. The card is handed over, along with the words, 'Hello this is my card. You've been so good. Please come to my restaurant and I'll give you a glass of champagne at the bar.' Easy does it; you must be careful not to offer a job overtly, and you must leave yourself a way out should you change your mind. Recently I was at Scott's, the great fish restaurant in Mayfair. The service was amazing. I could have given my card to all the staff, but I didn't.

There is always the worry that one of your staff will leave and, in the process, take other staff with them to the next restaurant. It might be nice to poach, but it is certainly not nice to be poached from. When Michele, my assistant manager, left Galvin at Windows he said, 'Don't worry, I'm taking nobody.' True to his word, when other staff phoned him – 'Can I come to join you?' – they received a polite but brief response from Michele: 'I'm not taking you.' That is the kind of respect and love you don't get from many people. People like Michele are rare and special.

There was one member of my team who left and as soon as he was out of the door he started calling my staff, trying to poach them. Then he got a phone call from me. I said, 'Listen, you know this is not good, this is not on. If you carry on there will be trouble, so stop, or else...' The poaching stopped. I am not sure what trouble I could have caused: there is no law that gives me the authority to prevent poaching. But of course good managers want good staff, and they'll go out of their way to find them. You just have to use the right tactics. To defend yourself against poaching the key is to have extremely good working conditions and a happy atmosphere together with an open and honest relationship with your staff, who can then get on with the most important part of the business: that first line of defence.

I've never found a better comparison to the service industry than a battle. There are many others, but this is the one I always return to.

6

FLYING KNIVES AND STOLEN SPOONS

You do not begin life at a great restaurant with no experience in the restaurant trade. Or rather, if you do manage to sneak in and get a job, then you might not last more than a week. The road to the top is frequently a long and arduous one. Stars, as they say, must be earned.

Often that road starts with the season. That is when you work, just for the summer months, in a restaurant, resort or hotel that is at its busiest when the weather is hot and the entire world seems to be on holiday. The entire world, except for you, the waiter or chef. This sort of work is hard and sleep is scarce, but the pay can be exceptionally rewarding. When the tourists return home, the job becomes redundant. The season is over. Next year, you can 'do the season' again, should you wish and if you have the stamina.

The season has no geographical boundaries and is not

confined to the Continent. If you are British, you might find yourself spending a few summer months as a waiter or chef in a restaurant or hotel – or even a fish and chip shop – somewhere on the south coast or in Devon or Cornwall. If you are French or Italian, then you could end up in the South of France, or in Naples. Once you are at your destination, working the season, you will not leave until it is over. So take my advice, and choose a nice place.

The season is an ideal way to gain experience and knowledge, and to overdose on fun and partying. During the season you will exist in a sort of fantasy bubble. But within a matter of months that bubble will burst and you will be back in the humdrum of reality. Which is perfect because if the bubble did not burst – if the season did not come to an end – there's a chance you might die from exhaustion, alcohol poisoning or worse.

I can still recall my first day of my first season at the Monte Carlo Beach, a large five-star hotel just on the edge of Monte Carlo and Roquebrune. The place was unbelievable, and had served the highest of high society ever since the hotel opened back in 1929. The car park was lined and shined with Ferraris, Lotuses, Bentleys and Mercs. The dining room was not, in fact, a room, but a sunny, expansive, terracotta-floored terrace, with neatly placed gazebos for guests who wanted to avoid melting in the blazing heat.

Luxurious sun loungers surrounded the massive, glittering swimming pool, beside which cold drinks were served. Most of the people had come to eat and drink, and to 'chill' beneath the sun and the swaying palms, immersed in the scents of towering pines and smouldering Gitanes. The others were there to serve the people who had come to eat, drink and chill. So it was an interesting mixture of those who were relaxing and those who were working.

One of the waiters was a veteran who had notched up quite a few seasons at the Monte Carlo Beach. As we went for a drink one evening after work he whispered, 'Fred, look at the people who come on holiday here and remember their faces.'

'Why?'

'Because in a few months you'll see one or two of them on the news for tax evasion, murder, or robbery.'

I was working at the Société des Bains de Mer (SBM), which is owned by Monaco's royal family and controls hotels and casinos in the principality. I was part of the Brigade Volante, the Flying Squad, and we formed the staff of six or seven major venues during the summer months. There was an events venue, The Sporting Club, and this, in turn, was home to La Salle des Étoiles, a massive banqueting suite.

I had landed the job thanks to Monsieur Filipi, a cookery teacher at my college in Souillac. 'Monsieur Filipi, I want to buy a car, and in order to buy a car, I need a job. Please can you help me get a job?' I had my heart set on a Renault 5.

'Okay,' he said, 'I'll get you a job in Monte Carlo. Go for the season.' No problem. Monsieur Filipi was true to his word; he made a call, and that is how I came to be there in 1991, having my sleeve tugged by a seasoned waiter as I stood beside a huge swimming pool.

In two months I would earn the equivalent of £3,000, an enormous amount of money for a young man at that time. As I was indeed young and quite inexperienced, though very eager, I was paired up with a chef de rang called Jacques as his helper.

Jacques amassed a fortune in tips. In fact, every fortnight he made the equivalent of around £1,000 in gratuities. It was up to the chef de rang to divide the tips with his waiter – in this case, me. Of his £1,000, Jacques gave me £50. You might think that I got a bum deal but, although my takings were merely a fraction of his takings, I was happy with the cash. Others in my position received more, but some got nothing in tips, not a sous.

The beauty of La Salle des Étoiles was that at 11 o'clock at night the roof opened to reveal the sky and the stars. I was in awe. There were firework displays in the nearby harbour, and the sky lit up with explosions of colour. It was as if every day was Bastille Day, the national day of France. And beneath the stars, the guests watched cabaret performed by real-life stars such as Paul Anka, Harry Belafonte, Shirley MacLaine and the cherished French singer, Johnny Hallyday.

At La Salle, service started at 7pm and we had two hours to serve a three-course meal. The kitchen was 100m from the tables, so it was a case of running at considerable speed to the kitchen, and then returning just as quickly. Service was old school, so we didn't just carry plates with food on, oh no! The dishes were plated at the table. We would carry a stack of cloched dishes known as *la suite* from the kitchen. It was a balancing act – there was a tray, then the meat or fish, topped with a cloched dish of vegetables, then the sauce on top of all the plates. it was heavy! Sprinting waiters were a frequent sight.

Once you reached the table, you served the customers from the guéridon, a trolley or small table at which waiters finish a dish for the guests at the table. It takes its name from the guéridon table, which is small and round and was fashionable in France during the reign of Louis XIV. For guéridon service, the most senior waiter carves the meat or slices the fish; his junior serves the vegetables and pours over the sauce. The senior waiter then places the plate in front of the guest. As a commis, I was plating the vegetables and pouring the sauce.

Before the 'big act' came on stage, the audience was entertained by dancers wearing very little clothing and with legs that went on forever. There was a fine art to sprinting with la suite while resisting the temptation to glance at the dancers on stage.

The resort also had a casino, a bar and a restaurant called Le Maóna, which was Lebanese. The Hôtel de Paris had a roof terrace restaurant, appropriately enough called Le Terrace. The rota moved the staff from one place to another. So I might find myself setting up at the beach in the morning and serving lunch there, and at night-time I could be serving in La Maóna, or in the large, starry-skied banqueting room, where shifts tended to end particularly late. Luckily, I worked mostly at lunchtime the Monte Carlo Beach, which was the best place to work, or at the restaurant on the roof.

I wore a uniform of black trousers and a white shirt, emblazoned with a blue motif. I loved that shirt. I loved it so much that 15 years later I was still wearing it.

At the Monte Carlo we had to have the tables ready for service by noon. There were 6– 10 tables in each station, and it was imperative to look out for yourself. For instance, I had to ensure I had cutlery when it was necessary. Odd though it may sound, there was actually not enough cutlery to go around. This was partly because the staff stole it to take home, and partly and partly because some ended up in the bin as waiters cleared their plates in the bins in the back of house. So we learned to live with what was left, and to be clever. Each waiter had to prevent the others from stealing his essential cutlery.

A guest might ask, 'Bring me a spoon, please.' This may seem like a simple request, but in fact it could be a task of Herculean proportions. A waiter had to know where to find a spoon at all times, which meant guarding cutlery so that it never went missing. This is a peculiar boast, but I was never without a spoon or a ladle, a fork or a glass. A ship's captain has his logbook, a policeman has his handcuffs. We had our cutlery.

Throughout the day, there was a constant refrain:

'Excuse me, do you have a spoon?'

'No, I'm sorry Madame, I don't have any spoons.'

Or you would see a waiter pleading with another waiter. 'Please can I have some spoons? If I don't have spoons, I can't serve coffee.'

'Sorry, I have no spoons.'

When I was doing my *mise en place* – preparing the tables in my station or section – I kept a close eye on that cutlery. If another waiter was late he was foolish because he would discover he had no cutlery ... and soon he would have no scruples. He would swoop in, pinch everything and put it in his station, on his tables. You could lay the tables so that they looked positively pristine, complete with glasses, knives, forks and spoons. Ten minutes later, all of it could have been removed by a devious waiter and placed on several nearby tables. I say nothing of mine ever went missing. Actually, it did happen once, but it never happened again.

Each waiter did his mise en place and then stood, watching

the tables, ready to pounce if another waiter swooped in to pinch knives, forks, spoons and/or glasses. During service I learned to be fast, serving the guests but keeping an eye out, just to check my spoons were safe.

I kept ladles hidden behind foliage in large flower pots. Competition was fierce, even though we were working in the same restaurant, for the same damn cause.

Then there was the kitchen. Within a couple of shifts, I had the measure of the way it worked. The head chef and his buckled stove were both about 60 years old, and I went into the kitchen, saying, 'Chef, the guest on table eight wants his food now. He needs it now. Chef! Chef! Chef!' The chef looked me up and down. He glared. 'Shut up. Get to back of the queue, as you would in the brothel!' You can fill in the additional expletives as you wish, and then add a few more. The insults from the chef came thick and fast, each one delivered in a hellish, deafening roar. On the other side of the swing doors, the guests were in paradise, eating, drinking, giggling and relaxing. They could relish the tranquillity beside the pool, on the terrace or in the shade of gazebos. Looking back, the jangling music of the cheerful steel band served a significant purpose, helping to drown out the rage, the swearing and the shouting from Chef.

And while Chef shouted, waiters on the other side of the pass were asking themselves: 'How can I jump the queue? How can I avoid being attacked by this monster? How can I become a friend of this hollering beast?'

The kitchen is also where I discovered tomato and mozzarella. I had never eaten it before. Every day I would make an order for tomato and mozzarella, just as if a guest had ordered it. Then, after service, I would collect the dish from the kitchen, whisk it off to a quiet place and promptly eat it. Others knew I was doing it, but they were doing it too, not necessarily with tomato and mozzarella. All of these dishes that were eaten by the waiters were charged to the guests. I'm ashamed to admit it, but that was then and that was how it was done, and not just in Monte Carlo.

Guests who came daily included a large, overweight Italian man. Nestled in his chest hair he wore a gold chain bearing ingots the size of pieces of Toblerone. Walking by his side were his wife and their son Giovanni, a boy of about five or six. I have never seen a boy take so many slaps from his father. In between the slaps there was a touch of fatherly generosity: when the boy wanted to buy an ice cream, his father would pull out a wad of cash – 'Here you go' – and hand him brand new 500 franc note. I know the ice creams were expensive but perhaps not that expensive!

But there would be moments at the Monte Carlo Beach when I was more concerned about my colleagues who were serving than I was about the guests. One example was Dinesh. He was from Sri Lanka and was in charge of the drinks dispenser at this jewel on the Riviera. When I first said hello to him I had noticed his eyes were bloodshot and unfocused. These were the effects, I quickly learned, of the mind-numbing amounts of marijuana that he smoked. When he was not busy, he would play around with a carving knife, twirling it in the air, and smiling as he just about functioned in his spaced out zone.

Pierre who came from the French Alps was, like me, another young waiter. He was a bit of a joker, but his jokes were not always well received, and on one occasion he caused particular offence when he made a reference to Dinesh's sexuality. It was just a casual joke, but Dinesh was about a metre away, standing behind the drinks counter, eyes bloodshot, knife in hand. What happened next happened in a flash. I shall never forget it. Dinesh raised the knife and threw it at Pierre. A split-second later, the lengthy blade was protruding from the wall a mere hand's breadth from Pierre's head. His face had turned green and the smile had been wiped clean off it.

I still cannot believe how lucky he was not to have been injured. Pierre yelled at Dinesh, 'Are you mad? Why did you do this? Can you imagine if you'd missed?' Dinesh replied slowly (he was stoned, remember), 'I never miss. Now don't you ever mess with me again. Get lost or else!'

Pierre scurried away. He never again bothered Dinesh. There were no repercussions: HR were not involved and the incident was not reported to the manager. Or, if he did know, he never did anything about it. Rumour had it that Dinesh was actually a gangster back in Sri Lanka.

I learned pretty quickly that the abuse of alcohol and drugs in this warm, idyllic spot, beside the ever-lapping waves of the Mediterranean, was commonplace, and more so among the staff than the clientele.

I was 18 years old and this was my introduction to the season. I would like to say I know of no knife-throwing incidents in restaurants since then, but that would not be true. A few years ago I heard about a sous chef who threw a knife at a waiter across the pass. It was in the kitchen of a multi-award-winning restaurant in the UK. I was appalled to learn the chef was not dismissed.

At one in the morning, when our work was done, it was time for us to party. We hit the bars and the clubs. Every member of staff wore sunglasses, partly to protect us from the bright glare of daylight, but also because we were so tired. As I mentioned earlier, sleep during the season is a rarity.

One day I was working but felt shattered from a succession of sleepless nights and hedonism. I sneaked a quick break from the tables and popped into the bathroom. As I stood in front of the mirror I lifted my sunglasses – I suppose I wanted to see how bad my eyes looked. Would they be as bloodshot as Dinesh's? 'My God,' I said to myself. 'What the hell has happened?' It was not what I saw; the problem was that I couldn't see anything. I was literally blind with exhaustion. Momentarily panicked, I turned on the taps and splashed water on my face until I could see again.

Our accommodation was a three-storey building overseen by a sort of housemaster who had been a sergeant in the army. My room overlooked the sea, and my work was close: the Monte Carlo Beach, the Sporting Club and the beach were all less than half a kilometre away. When I met an English girl at the hotel's pool, I invited her back to my room, but this was against the rules. Fortunately our housemaster was open to bribes – bottles of whisky – which kept everyone happy and meant I got even less sleep.

The rooms in the block were pretty filthy. Many were home to Italian men, aged between 35 and 50, who came every season to work at the hotel, drawn like bees to honey – or money. One of the rooms was occupied by a group of gay men, one of whom was tall and flamboyant, and he paraded around the building in his white Y-fronts. 'Oh, Fred, what are you doing?

Do you have time to give me a massage?' Erm, no, I did not.

Within these dirty walls, the fun was endless: sex, drugs, drink. Drugs were on tap – acid, weed, coke. The staff had left their homes and their real lives well behind them and they were thinking, 'I can do whatever I like.' And they did. Anything goes in the South of France in the summer, and indeed, anything did. For many, sleep began at 6am. Work, meanwhile, began shortly afterwards, at 9am. When we finished at four o'clock in the afternoon, many of us went to the beach, where we slept before the next shift. I would have a shower, brush my teeth, go to work, have a coffee and – hey presto! – I felt awake. When the season was over, it took me a mere three months to recover.

Obviously, we were in the midst of casino culture. The guests spent their time gambling at the tables, but so too did some of the waiters and kitchen staff. It was not unusual to see a colleague, the despondent look of gloom etched on his face. 'I've lost it all,' he would say. But he would be able to earn more cash very quickly, and be able to lose it even faster, after a spin or two of a roulette wheel.

———

The general manager, or GM, and his two lieutenants always sat at a table at the Sporting Club, and to me, they looked like Mafia dons. I admired them hugely, and never could have imagined that I would be sitting in their place one day. You did not approach them unless they beckoned you over. You did not speak to them unless spoken to. Early on, a chef de rang and pointed at the GM, saying, 'What he says, goes.' The GM was the top boss and if you didn't know the top boss, or if you didn't know somebody who knows somebody who knows somebody who knows the top boss, then you didn't work there.

The guests, meanwhile, were big tippers. People do not tip anymore, especially in Britain, what with the service charge and the confusion over what is service charge and what is a tip. However, in France a tip is *pour boire*: for a drink. When the plumber comes over to fix your leaks, you might pay him a few hundred pounds and then give him a tenner for a drink. There is no confusion there. But for waiting staff, the British customer is unsure. The bill arrives and the guest thinks, 'I don't know, has the waiter already got the service, or not?'

In those days, in Monte Carlo, there was no confusion. The guests were generous. They paid the bill, paid the service charge and then they left a tip, the equivalent of £50 or £100. Nowadays, if you get £50 it's a big thing. Back then, £50 was not an unusual tip at the Monte Carlo Beach. We did not work for the tip but we knew it was coming and it was part of the job and a necessity: tips enabled us to live, save up . . . and party! Thanks to my teacher, Monsieur Filipi, my time at the Monte Carlo Beach enabled me to buy that car. It was a Renault 5, a snip at the equivalent of £3,000.

The guests were also as self-indulgent as the staff. There were waiters who drank during service but, as you can imagine, the guests also enjoyed the alcohol (and did not need to hide it). I still recall a couple in their fifties who were very friendly, chatting to me, all smiles and laughter. Pointing to the couple, I said to another waiter, 'I love these people. They're so sweet and nice.'

He said, 'Yeah, in a minute they're going to ask you to have sex with them.' I laughed off the suggestion. But it turned out my colleague was not joking. As the gentleman and his wife were about to leave the table, they asked, 'Would you like to join us for a drink tonight?' Along with the invitation there were plenty of winks, giggles and innuendo – from them, not me. The inference was clear. They were predators, out for young flesh and that young flesh happened to be mine.

'I'm sorry,' I said, flattered. 'It's not my type of thing.' Off the couple went, weaving away, in search of another, more accommodating young waiter.

The season taught me how to get away with all sorts of behaviour: where to hide the spoons, yes, but also how to maintain excellence in the face of adversity (and a massive hangover!).

7

THE TABLE

The table. A simple structure: a flat piece of wood balanced on four legs. At home, we treat it casually and at mealtimes we usually throw down some mismatched knives and forks (with chipped handles), and use kitchen roll as paper napkins.

In any good restaurant, however, the look and the feel of the tables are paramount to customer satisfaction and ultimately they contribute to the popularity and success of a restaurant. And so they should! The surface of the table is like an artist's canvas that starts out blank and is gradually filled in. To set a table to restaurant standard is a professional skill, and one that I am proud to have worked hard at and mastered. As you will see, a table is never just a table in a restaurant; it is the sum of many different aspects and much careful work.

From my early childhood, I was the table setter. Before every meal at home, as my mother cooked in the kitchen, my job was to set the table – and to set it properly. So, even before I began a life in service, I had a proper appreciation for a well-laid table. Onto the table went the plates, cutlery, linen napkins, a jug of water and glasses, as well as bread and, as is the French way, wine. It is possible that more often than not I put the fork on the right rather than the left. Setting the table was as much of a ritual for me as it was for Pierre, my brother, to head off to the loo and stay there until I had completed the task. A loo would then flush and Pierre would emerge for the meal. He managed to dodge table duties for years. He was a bit lazy back then, but he is my younger brother so all is forgiven.

Once everything was finished, Pierre would return to the little boys' room while I cleared the table, loaded the dishwasher and washed the pots and pans. Having been trained by my father, I did not merely wipe the table but cleaned it thoroughly with a steaming-hot sponge, ensuring there was not a crumb or a smear left behind. I cleaned the underside of the table, before washing the sponge in hot water and giving the surface a final wipe over. I would rinse the sponge, put it to one side of the sink, and then meticulously wash and dry my hands like a surgeon. Only then was my task completed, and Pierre could come back from the loo.

That was how things were during my childhood. Things changed at catering college, and I have to confess that during my first year I did not know how to set a table because I could never remember where to place the fork and where to place the knife. Pretty basic knowledge for you, perhaps, but for me it was always a source of deep confusion. For some reason my brain simply could not retain the information. One weekend I saw my aunt Nicole, and she asked how I was enjoying catering college. I said 'It's great, but I can never remember whether the fork goes on the left or the right.' In a flash, Aunt Nicole solved the problem. She pressed her left hand to the left side of her chest and told me, 'All you need to remember is that the fork goes on the side of your heart.' That's how I've remembered it ever since.

Of course, there is so much more to learn than simply where to put the fork. The next important lesson is that setting the table is not enough; in fact you cannot start with the table. You have to start with the whole dining room. First, you must ensure that the room is clean: every surface dusted, every light bulb spotless. Take a step back, and look at the room; you want perfect symmetry, harmony, and balance – the Japanese garden all over again.

It is not enough to have a clean dining room. You must also know your dining room: a clear understanding of the table plan for the service ahead is essential before you even think about the table. Each table is placed both in relation to the other tables and the other chairs, but also in relation to where the guests will come from and whether they will be able to sit down without disturbing others at their tables, or at the tables around them. This may sound obvious, but you would be surprised at how few restaurants really pay attention to this. No matter how many tables you have, and how big your room is, in every restaurant, there is always a prime position for each and every table. Now, should the table be round, square or rectangular? I do not have a preference, but over the years I have noticed that people certainly seem to 'connect' better when they are seated at a round one.

There has to be enough space for the guests to move around

the table so that they can get to and from their chairs, and so that they can move their chairs in and out in a way that does not inconvenience other guests. There also has to be sufficient room for the waiters to be able to carry out service, comfortably passing around the table and guests. And never forget: just as a hotel does not have thirteenth floor, a restaurant does not have a table 13. Who would want to sit at table 13? (Bowing to the restaurateur's superstition, there is no Chapter 13 in this book.)

When I worked at Le Gavroche there was one table that needed particular attention. Table Nine was big and close to the kitchen, and annoyingly it was also very near a pillar, which meant that during service it was difficult to serve the guests on the pillar-end of the table. So, before you even started to set the table, you had to make sure the table was exactly the right distance from the end of the pillar. But frequently, we waiters forgot to make absolutely certain, and every evening, shortly before service, Silvano, the maître d', would start shouting 'What's wrong with you guys? Look at this table. Look how you've set it up. Can't you see it's too close to the pillar? Can't you just set it to make sure it's aligned?' Thank goodness for his care. He knew that leaving it incorrectly aligned would mean big problems in the middle of a busy service!

Poor positioning of a table is a basic and common mistake. It drives me crazy when one of my waiters puts the table too close to an ice bucket. This can be very dangerous. A guest might push his chair back and knock the bucket, causing the ice and water to spill all over the floor, which would be a major distraction during service. An ice bucket in the wrong place represents a failure to master the simple basics of how to set up the table and consider the consequences of your actions.

So, now the table is in the right place, what next? Is the table well balanced and secure or is it unsteady? A wobbly table is not acceptable. And you must not forget the chairs. When you sit on the chair is it relaxing? Does it feel secure, or have the springs gone and is an arm loose? Next, the undersides of the table and chairs have to be checked. There are times, I am sorry to say, when guests put chewing gum – or worse – under their seats. I have also worked in restaurants where guests have placed small pieces of uneaten food, or even bits they have chewed, found not to their taste and spat out, under the arms or seats of their chairs or on the underside of tables. Less unhygienic but no less hazardous, there may also be splinters of wood lurking under chairs or tables. You do not want the guests to discover any of this, so before they arrive you must conduct your own search by running your fingers under each table and chair to make sure they are clean. The things we do!

Once this is done, wash your hands thoroughly, because now it is time for the white linen tablecloth. This custom is known as 'clothing the table', and each table must be consistently clothed – balance, symmetry, beauty. It has become fashionable to do away with the white linen. The restaurateur who does not have tablecloths is, of course, spared the expense of buying them and then having them laundered on a daily basis. In many restaurants white linen does not suit the style of the place or the cuisine. Think of those restaurants that serve great Japanese ramen, Chinese noodles or Spanish tapas. White linen tablecloths do not tend to feature regularly. This makes perfect sense: imagine the cleaning – ramen, noodles and tapas, no matter how exceptional, can be fast food, eaten swiftly. White linen transports you to a place where time does not matter; you can linger all you want; we are prepared and ready for you to do so. It takes you back to the days before the internet, smart phones and the frantic rush of life. A symbol of quality, relaxation and luxury, white linen brings a little bit of softness to a restaurant's environment.

It is not just enough for a tablecloth to be clean. It has to be crisp and properly ironed, At Galvin at Windows, very occasionally, if a cloth is badly creased, we will lay it onto the table and then iron it. But by and large this is unnecessary; laundries have upped their standards and we have the best in the business. In France, the three-star Michelin restaurants still uphold the tradition of ironing the cloths on the table, to make absolutely certain that there are no creases. A friend of mine worked at the Louis XV, Alain Ducasse's restaurant in Monte Carlo, and they were even more fastidious than that. When the cloths came back from the laundry, already spotless and already perfectly ironed, they were placed on special hangers, designed to prevent them creasing. Then, once the cloths had been laid on the table, they were ironed once more by a commis. The kind of detail employed by Ducasse's team makes me think of a grand house in the 1900s, and how they would have looked after the linen. It is an astonishing level of attention to detail and I take my hat off to them.

Once the cloth is on the table, the fold should be at exactly the same height at each corner of the table; there cannot be a corner that is folded more than another. It should hang down about 20–30cm from the tabletop. Flowers are then placed on the table, along with the salt and pepper (if you use them) –

aligned to perfection. Flowers are expensive and you have to look at what you have in the budget, but they add vibrancy and beauty, especially when in season. I say 'if you use them' for salt and pepper because I have chosen not to at Galvin at Windows. Salt and pepper is only given upon request. Our chef Joo Won seasons each dish perfectly, so there is no need to have them on the table. It saves us time, labour and money, and it makes a confident statement.

———⊨

The chairs are now placed around the table so that they are equidistant from one another. If it is a table for four, and there are 20cm between two chairs, there will also be 20cm between the other two. The chairs must also be flush to the table. In other words, the hand end of the chair's arms should be aligned and beside the tablecloth at the point where it falls at the edge of the table. The reason is logical: it enables you, the waiter, to imagine and take into consideration where the guest would be. Therefore it provides a very accurate indication of the space the guest will have once he or she is seated. You can establish, for instance, whether two chairs on neighbouring tables will touch each other. If those chairs are back to back, you know exactly what space you have.

Every chair at the table has a position number. This relates to the position of the guest at the table, so that when the dishes are brought to the table you do not need to ask which guest is having which dish because you know the position. This is established when you take the order from each guest. You write down, for example, 'Beef – 1. Dover sole – 2.' and so on.

How do the members of staff know the position of each chair? Well, when you open the restaurant you decide on the positioning. So, for example, some restaurants will say that the chair closest to the front door is position one. Others will say that the chair closest to the kitchen will be position one. Others will decide the chair closest to the terrace is position one. Once you have position one at the table, the other position numbers move clockwise around the table.

If plates are to be used in the table setting, these are known as *les assiettes de mise en place*. They are next to go onto the table, and the first plate is placed right at the centre of the first position. Then you work around the table clockwise. The next step is to place a napkin in front of each imaginary guest, again beginning at position one and working clockwise. Remembering that all-important symmetry, each napkin is placed on the table – dead centre – above the plate. To do this correctly, think of the middle of the chair: the napkin should be precisely equidistant between each side of the chair. If the chair is 40cm wide, the napkin should be exactly in the middle. Therefore, if the napkin is 20cm wide, there should be 10cm of space on either side, making it symmetrical.

There are many ways to fold napkins, and you can choose whichever one you prefer. I follow the code that the napkin – and the tablecloth – should be touched as little as possible. The more you touch what goes onto the table, the greater the risk that cross-contamination might occur when the guests also come into contact with it. Sometimes you do see a particularly well-folded napkin, which is pretty and uplifting. But the intricate folding means that the waiter has had to touch it ten or 20 times with his hands, so I would not recommend it. Instead, I like a napkin that is simply folded, thereby eliminating repeated contact, no matter how clean your hands are. Another bugbear of mine is when waiters clear a table and put their fingers in the wine glasses to carry them away. Then they come to your table, bringing the plates, which they touch with their fingers – and they have not washed their hands in between.

Once the napkins have been positioned, you place the knives on the table. Not the forks. The knife goes to the right of the plate. To avoid smudges and poor hygiene, hold the knife by the side of the handle, between your thumb and index finger. Do not put your thumb or finger on the blade of the knife. To attain perfect symmetry, stand behind the chair and lean over it to place the knife, so that you can see exactly what you are doing from the guest's point of view and make sure it is right. The distance between the plate, or the napkin, and the knife should be a thumb's width.

The knife is laid first because in the high-class restaurants of the old days there would always be a sommelier, and he was the one in charge of putting the glasses on the table before service. To place them correctly he used the positioning of the knife. The wine glass is put straight above the knife, so there are about 2 or 3cm of space, depending on the house. The water glass is placed to the side of the wine glass, but at a slight angle.

Next, the fork, which goes to the left of the napkin – the side of your heart, as Aunt Nicole told me. You do the same with the fork as you did for the knife: holding it correctly and placing it a thumb's width from where the plate will be set down. After positioning the fork, comes the side plate. This is put on the table, about 2cm from the plate. It is there for the bread, and is about a thumb's distance or two (depending on the service) to the left of the fork. The top of the side plate should follow an imaginary line that runs from the top of the fork and the top of the knife. The bread knife is placed on top the side plate. Again, ensure that the two knives and the fork are aligned and parallel.

When you are setting the table, you are not only setting it up perfectly for a single cover. Visual balance is applied once again: each cover must match the others on that table. Four covers, for instance, must be completely symmetrical. To do the job well, you must create a mirror image. For a table of six, positions three and six will be mirrored, positions two and five will be mirrored, and so on.

Before table-setting, all the cutlery and glasses must be cleaned and polished to a shine. Double-check that the cutlery is spaced wide enough apart so that there is no need to move it when the plates are put on the table in front of each guest. The type of plate depends on the style of the restaurant. Should they be round, square, oval or even chopping boards? The answer is that there must be a balance between aesthetics, practicality and the smooth running of a restaurant.

Oddly shaped plates can add a bit of interest for the guest, but for the waiting staff (and also for the chefs) they can add a level of complexity to the service. They can also be difficult to store, so you need to consider all these things, and it would be unwise to buy a lot of plates without carefully considering how they will fit in with service. Ask yourself, do they truly add value? Sometimes they can be a nightmare: you cannot store them, they break easily or are difficult to place on the table.

Table-setting takes practice to perfect and might seem laborious and fiddly, but not to the perfect host. Also, it can be fun as I discovered when working at La Salle des Étoiles. We had to set up scores of tables, and each waiter had a role in the process. One waiter was in charge of laying the tablecloth, another placed the knives, another the forks, and yet another waiter placed the napkins and so on. Sometimes the mise en place team was led by an utterly mad and very funny Italian chef de rang, Antonino. When we were setting up the tables he would make it into a race. We would all be on the same team racing towards a common goal – to set up the whole room in world-record time. Although we did not race each other per se you had to keep up with Antonino or whoever was one step ahead of you.

And Antonino was fast! In order to keep up we would run around the tables, each waiter speedily performing his role: the tablecloth, the napkin, the knife, glass, fork, side plate … Antonino was the race master, and usually in charge of laying the tablecloths, as well as being the one beating the drums like they used to on Roman galleys. We could transform a table from totally empty to completely set at a machine-gun pace. Rat-a-tat-tat!

These days I am not in the habit of making my waiters race round tables (this would be unseemly) but there is always the opportunity for some fun in the proceedings: as long as it ends up perfect, of course!

8

—●≣

LA CLEM

Racing around setting tables was far from my mind during my second season. This time I was working at the Hotel Royal in La Baule-Escoublac, on a pretty part of the coast of Brittany in Northern France. In the summer months, Baule, with its long stretch of white sand, becomes a popular seaside resort in the west of France, full of Parisians and tourists from the nearby city of Nantes. They all needed food and a bed for the night, and so they came to this hotel, if they could afford it. It was large, grand and luxurious: the archetypal five-star institution.

—●≣

When I first arrived I was bossed around mercilessly by the maître d'hôtel. He drove a Citroën 2CV, was extremely volatile and was a terrible boss. I distinctly remember the 2CV because, during my time there, the maître d' sacked a member of the staff for some reason or another. The disgruntled employee left the hotel and returned shortly afterwards, carrying a sledgehammer, which used to smash the Citroën almost to smithereens. The police were called and inspected the battered and dented vehicle, but in the end there was no evidence to incriminate the ex-employee. Perhaps someone else held a grudge – I wouldn't be surprised!

I was there to do restaurant service, but the maître d' put me to work in the banqueting suite, where my chores included carting around heavy piles of plates and enormous boxes of glasses. I was also ordered to assemble and reassemble hundreds of chairs around tables. I did not like any of it. The boss was treating me like an unpaid intern, known as *stagiaires*. These are the lowest of the low, and are usually lumbered with all the worst jobs and most menial tasks.

I went to complain to the maître d'. 'Monsieur, I am sorry but I will have to call my school. I am not here to do this donkey work.' I made such a fuss that … it worked! He transferred me to the beach restaurant, which is precisely where I wanted to be. Wouldn't you? And at the end of the two-month placement the maître d' presented me with a glowing report.

There was a chef at this hotel who was 26, but he looked 40 because he drank so much wine. The guests, meanwhile, included a wealthy, elderly Parisian lady, who spent six months of the year in the hotel. Madame Clementine was known to the staff (though not to her face) as 'La Clem'. 'Elle peuke,' we would all say (again, not to her face), she stinks. She smelled musty, as if her clothes had not been washed for some time.

La Clem would emerge from her room only to come down

to the hotel's beach restaurant for lunch. If she ate breakfast or dinner, then she did so in her room. Every lunch she ate alone and I do not recall her ever having visitors. For lunch and for dinner she ordered langoustines and mayonnaise. That is all she ate – langoustines and mayonnaise. Then she would return to her room and stay there for the rest of the day.

La Clem could have been a hundred for all I knew, and she may well have been suffering from dementia. At every meal, she was given a quiet table in the far side of the room, thereby sparing other guests from the smell. Once seated, she would peruse the menu as if, today, she fancied something different. The maître d' would go to her table to take the order and each time the following scene took place:

'Madame, how charming you look today. What would you like? Have you decided?'

'Oh,' she would reply. 'I don't know what I'm going to have. Erm … I think today I shall have the langoustines, please.'

'Langoustines, Madame?'

'Yes, please. And mayonnaise.'

'Bien sûr, Madame,' said the maître d', writing down the order. 'Certainement.'

It was the same every day for six months. Langoustines and mayonnaise. Then she would return to Paris and I still wonder what she ate every day at home in the French capital.

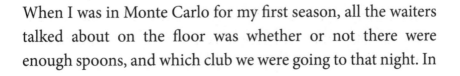

When I was in Monte Carlo for my first season, all the waiters talked about on the floor was whether or not there were enough spoons, and which club we were going to that night. In this second season, we still talked about the clubs but we also talked about La Clem.

In a good restaurant, 99 per cent of the time waiters on the floor discuss the sequence and events of service. There is never time to chat for long, so it is fast-paced communication and to the point. Has the water been served? Has the wine been poured? They check whether or not an order has been taken. Then there is the silent communication between the waiting staff. Quite simply, you keep an eye on each other and on the guests to gauge that they are enjoying their meal and the experience, and that everything is running smoothly. You watch out, for instance, to see if a guest has dropped a napkin on the floor. Or whether a child is eating his or her meal or if it is time to take them into the kitchen for some ice cream – a moment of excitement for any youngster.

All of this is about customer experience and how to deliver it without fail because, I can assure you, the greatest satisfaction does not happen by chance. You need to communicate with your colleagues all the time and, as I said, this communication is not always verbal. In a good restaurant, the waiting staff will be alert, looking and thinking about the same thing, which is the pursuit of pleasing the guest and delivering excellent service.

The remaining 1 per cent of the time waiters discuss frivolous things. We might talk about something unrelated to the business, such as politics, and I must admit we also joke about the guests, having fun at their expense.

The restaurant business, I think, is a bit like the world of boxing: it is a profession that accepts anyone. Everybody on the team is welcomed, and nothing is off limits in terms of conversation. You feel very much at ease, and feel like opening up … and you do.

If there is a beautiful guest at a table, it is highly likely a waiter will make a comment about him or her – hopefully out of earshot. The waitresses talk about this kind of thing just as much as the waiters. What is amusing is that these asides take place in the middle of the floor when the waiters and waitresses are all smiles and tending to the guests' every need.

9

FOLLOWING THE ORDER

I've talked about the importance of preparing that first line of defence, and of having a perfectly prepared table, but all this can fall apart if you do not take the order properly. You must always keep your wits about you when you are taking an order from the guest. There might be special requirements, or food allergies that can be very serious and, in the worst cases, fatal. Whatever the situation, the job of a good waiter is to make sure that the food that ends up on the customer's table is exactly the food they ordered. And while this might seem like a given, we all know that things are never that simple.

You take the order and write the check neatly and carefully, sufficiently neatly that someone else would be able to read it quickly and easily if you happened to be called away. Any member of staff should be able to come onto the station and pick up where you left off. If you are in the trenches in the heat of battle, you know that when reinforcements arrive they will know exactly what to do. It is the same sort of thing in terms of service strategy: service goes extremely fast and anything can happen. Let's say someone is not performing and has forgotten to do a basic task, and when you point this out they burst into tears and run off … but you have to carry on; there are hungry mouths to feed.

Most restaurants now have an electronic system for relaying orders to the kitchen, called point of sale or POS, and so you write the order on the pad first, and then type the order onto a computer. Once you have typed in the order, you must cross-check it again with your handwritten note on the pad to make sure it is correct. Your handwritten pad should not only note how many of each dish, but which guest at which position is having what. The first number corresponds to the number of dishes, the second number is the position having the dish, 'Starter: 2 salmon, 1 and 4; 3 chicken, 2, 3 and 5; Main course: 2 beef medium, 1 and 5; 1 halibut, 4; 2 tagliatelle 2 and 3; 2 broccoli, 2 salad, 2 mash to share.' Then you press 'send' and you write down the time that you have sent it. This is important because it enables you to keep an eye on the timing of dishes: timing is absolutely key. Every guest has an in-built clock in his brain. Whether or not the guest has a watch, he or she will know instinctively if the food is late. Our stomachs are our best clocks. Time goes very quickly when you are in the middle of service. By noting the time you will know exactly what to expect and be prepared.

There are time periods in which a dish must be delivered – these differ from restaurant to restaurant, but every good restaurant should have one. At Galvin at Windows, a starter is typically 10–12 minutes from the point of order. A main course should arrive 15–20 minutes after the guest has finished the starter. The dessert should arrive 10–12 minutes after the main course has been finished. If each of these courses is not delivered within these times the customer starts to get fidgety.

The check goes to the kitchen and the chef reads it out aloud to the brigade: in service-talk, he 'calls' it. The relevant chefs then answer, 'Oui chef,' acknowledging they have heard and will start preparing the dish. In good kitchens all you hear is 'Oui chef'; nothing else. The chef then puts it on his check holder – a ruler with stickers – he marks it, and the cooking starts. Simultaneously the check is checked by the chef de passe.

Once the dish has been prepared, and the chef is happy with it, it goes onto the pass. As we already know, there are two sides to the pass. Each side will have a row of order tickets neatly printed out, ready for checking. The busboy that is carrying the dish to the table will check the dishes on the service side of the pass, making sure they match the check, and familiarising himself with where they need to go. For customers with allergies or special medical requirements, there may also be a special sticker next to the plate – implying that you need to make one more check before taking the dishes off the pass. No mistakes are allowed here!

The busboy now takes the dishes on a tray from the pass to the table. When he arrives at the table, he is met by you, the waiter, who will serve the food to the guests at the table. In some cases this could also be the manager. The waiter looks at the dishes and looks at the check – what is written on the check should match what is on the tray: '2 eggs, 2 eggs, table

4'. Another double-checking process to make sure the order is being met. If you are the one who has taken the order then you should know if it is correct. But let's say a different waiter comes in from another station because you are busy with a problem at another table. If the system is followed correctly, this waiter will be able to check quickly and efficiently that the order is correct, without needing to bother you. For VIP guests (or those with allergies) a manager may also make yet another check before the food is served. Whoever puts the dish down on the table is effectively the last line of defence. Although the dish should be perfect and has been prepared according to the guest's request because of the five checks that have already been carried out, you never know what difficulties may arise. All you know is that they will. It could be that the pass is being overseen by a sous chef who is not as good as the head chef. Or you have a chef at the pass who went out last night and is still a bit drunk and so forgot to put the garnish on the plate, the garnish that completes the dish. Or worse still, he has forgotten the main part of the dish altogether! Of course, it isn't always the fault of someone having too much fun the night before: there's always human error. We all make mistakes! The only defence any of us have is to check. And check. And check again. Always check the check. I call this positive paranoia, and I suffer from the condition more than anyone.

—◄

Allergies are, of course, the most important reason to get a check right. At Galvin at Windows, we have a system whereby an allergy is noted both on the handwritten pad and at the

POS, where 'allergy' is then typed into the electronic order system. In the kitchen, the chefs then know to put the dish on a separate part of the pass that is lined with a red piece of paper meaning 'Attention, allergy, you've got to be careful'. In addition to the electronic safeguard, whoever takes the order must verbally communicate the allergy to the kitchen, 'Chef, I just want to warn you that table four has an allergy. No nuts, no peanuts.' Then, when the dish is taken on a tray into the dining room, the allergy is also communicated to the waiter who will be taking the dishes and serving them at the table. They should ask:

'Is there an allergy?'

'Yes, it's guest position one – no nuts on one, but the rest of the party is okay.'

Of course, the waiter can also see the ticket, which tells him which table position has the allergy, so this is another way of checking that this is the correct dish. Then he can serve it to the right person according to the position at the table.

Is it foolproof? Nothing is, but this is as close as we will get. It relies on discipline, and if someone does not follow the procedure correctly, and ends up missing something, you have to come down very hard. I tell my team, 'Guys, remember, I have trained you in health and safety. You know what to do, the agreement you have signed, and that you are responsible. If anybody dies and you served the food, you will go to jail.' This may sound dramatic but people can die, so I take it very seriously indeed.

I have been aware of nut allergies throughout my career. But recently I have noticed increasing numbers of people with allergies to gluten or lactose intolerance. People will say at the beginning of the meal, 'Just so you know, I'm allergic to dairy products.' Of course, this isn't a problem: we can be flexible, and make arrangements. But when it comes to dessert, say they order the Tarte Tatin. You then say, 'Oh, just to let you know, Tarte Tatin comes with vanilla ice cream.' And the customer replies, 'Oh, I'm fine with vanilla ice cream.' Well, of course, if they are fine with ice cream, you do not need to be Sherlock Holmes to ascertain that he or she does not actually have an allergy. Rather, there is something they would prefer not to eat. Of course, the customer is king, and they do not have to tell us everything about themselves. But it is important to remember that even though there are 'allergies' and allergies: if somebody mentions the word, you must take note and be alert. You just never know. When I came to Britain 25 years ago we never had requests like this. People ate what was on the menu and there were very few who had allergies – maybe those who did never went out to restaurants – but I doubt it. In our restaurant now there is not a single service without ten, 12 or 15 'allergies'.

If an allergy goes unflagged, then this is one type of problem. There are plenty of other things that can go wrong. You could put a check through, via the POS, and somehow a technical fault means it does not go to the kitchen, or the check gets lost. What should you do? Well, it is always best to return to one of my favourite mottos: never leave a customer alone with his thoughts. Never ever be afraid to inform the guest that 'The starter's taking a bit longer than planned because there was a technical fault …' Let the guest know what is happening and why, before they start wondering for themselves. This way, you are able to prove that the customer is your absolute priority. When the dish is served, mention it again '… And there you are, Madame. Sorry for the delay. Enjoy.' And then followed, a moment later, by: 'Is everything all right?' You cannot necessarily control delays in service, but you can always control how you break the news to the customer. If the starter was late, which sometimes happens, you have to ensure that the main course is not as late, forcing you to apologise again. That is when you become a 'sorry' restaurant. 'Sorry Madame ... Sorry Sir ... Sorry about that ... Sorry about this ... Sorry about that ... Sorry, sorry, sorry, sorry, sorry.' Nothing can save you then.

I went out for dinner recently. It was a beautiful meal. Everything started incredibly well. It was the *dégustation* menu; wine with each course. The wine was served before my starter, just as it should be. Lovely. The second dish arrived, and once again the wine had already been served. The same was the case for the third dish. Then we came to the fish course and the wine was served two minutes after the plate was put in front of me. There had been a hiccup in service – the food was served first and the wine second. The dish was at the table and I turned around and saw the sommelier coming over with the wine. He was late. And the same thing happened for the next three courses.

At this particular restaurant they knew exactly what they had to do in order to be excellent. They knew the formula and I knew they knew it because they followed it for the first three dishes. But then for the second half of the meal the formula was forgotten, disregarded. They did it wrong once but this was not rectified – they kept on getting it wrong.

If this meal had been a football match, the home team would have been ahead at the end of the first half, but by the end of the second half they were in danger of losing the match as they kept missing opportunities to score.

The restaurant did not realise how many goals it missed out on. For me, the experience was lovely. The food was good, the wine was great, the company was amazing. The fact that I am talking about it means that my experience was not a ten out of ten; it was an eight out of ten. Would I go back? Yes. Do I believe that they are really, really good? No, I don't, because they lack focus. This could potentially lead to a drop in business and possibly closure, too, if they do not pick up their game.

Now, I may well be picky, but I think it is about professionalism and taking things to the nth degree. The waiter needs to second-guess what the guest will want before the guest even thinks of it. As the guest, I should not have to sit at the table, thinking, I have the food, but where is the wine? In this particular restaurant they did not second-guess me. And what is more, they should have fixed the problem because they had plenty of time – there were three or four other dishes still to be served. But they didn't. They left me alone with my thoughts wondering if and when the wines would be served with my dishes, and what is worse is that they did not even realise it.

This sort of repeated mistake can happen anywhere. I was in Galvin at Windows recently and observed one of the waitresses. At that time of the service all of the guests happened to be sitting on one side of the room. She walked past them, but she was looking in the opposite direction. I said, 'You are looking where there is nothing to see. You must be attentive and look at the guests … Look at the table, and at whether they're eating, or if they have they finished … Are their glasses empty? If you're looking in the wrong direction, you won't know the answers.' By saying this I think I alerted her to something very obvious, and hopefully this will provide a quick and easy solution to ensuring a better service. But we will see. I will keep watching her to see what she does. If she looks at the guests I will say, 'Well done, I'm glad that you took what I said on board,' because that will reinforce my message. If she does not do it right I will go back to her and say, 'Remember what I told you. This is what you need to do, so I want to see it.' Again, this will reinforce the message.

Boxing is one of my passions and many of the techniques and disciplines used in the sport can be applied – in theory – to service. Once I was talking to Nicola Adams, the British champion and I was feeling frustrated. I said, 'Nicola, sometimes I feel like I keep telling people the same thing over and over and over again. I just don't understand why they don't get it because they look at me and they say, "Yes, I want to do it. I want to get it, I'm getting it." But I keep having to tell them the same thing over and over because they're not doing it. This would be like them getting into the ring with someone and they've got their hands down. When the fight starts, their opponent throws a punch and splits their lip open – bam! So the trainer shouts, "Put your hands up." They put their hands up but the next minute they put them down again – bam! Now their nose is bleeding. They carry on, continuing to be hit until they put their hands up, or until they can't stay in the ring any longer.'

I said to Nicola, 'Do you understand? What do you do?' What can I do to get my managers and team to get it?

Nicola said, 'You keep punching them.'

I've tried to instil this level of care and attention into all my staff because you never know where the next blow will come from. Sometimes a member of staff does not turn up. Two people might be off sick and somehow you have to make sure that the rest of the staff can cover the floor so that none of the customers notice. People order wine that is not available because it has not been ordered from the wine supplier. Or they wanted the 2011 and they were given the 2013, and nobody lets them know that the vintage is out before opening the bottle, but they notice halfway through. All of these problems are easy to prevent if, collectively, you all have your guard up and are ready. With this mindset, you can prepare for the trickiest problem of all: the problem of taste.

Sometimes people do not like what is cooked for them. Quite literally, they do not like the food. They leave it because they do not like it. At this point, the waiter should be all over it, but that is not always the case. He should say, 'Is everything all right?'

'Yes, I'm just not hungry,' says the guest.

Now, as the waiter, are you satisfied with the answer? Or does it require a subtle nudge: 'Are you sure, Sir, it is just that you are not hungry … if it is not to your taste, I can get you something else if you want? That is not a problem.'

Even if they say no, and stick to their guns, it is kind to offer something and to show that you care and that you are prepared to go that little bit further. So just make sure and then take the plate away. But you have to ask twice – maybe three times – in a way that is not too forceful. You are just concerned, and rightly so, and are offering an alternative and showing that you are aware there might be a problem. This is such an easy thing to do, but very few waiters do it. It is all about judgement, and doing what is right then and there.

Taste is subjective, but sometimes things are just plain bad: the meat is cold and the sauce has congealed, or the vegetables are raw. Or everything is late, not just out of sync, but really, really late, and no one has apologised. Now, in either of these cases, should the guest complain? Well, I think the answer is never quite black and white. Say, for instance, that the food is a little late and no one warned you. If, when it arrives, it is delicious and you are happy now it is here, then you might decide that there's no point in complaining – you only wanted a main course anyway, and you just want to enjoy yourself.

But, as the one looking after guests, I always prefer to know if there is a problem. I want people to tell me if there is something wrong because I want to be able to deal with it before they leave the room. I want that chance to say, 'Look, I am very sorry. This is what happened ... I accept the error, it shouldn't be like this.' I want the chance to make it up to them, and learn from my mistakes to make sure it will not happen again.

How do you know when you have been given a genuine apology? Well, it should be instinctive. Your waiter should never shy away from apologising. There should be a drink or an invitation back to the restaurant 'as guests'. Above all, your complaint should be dealt with there and then, and this is when switched-on and attentive staff are absolutely essential. A complaint at the end of the meal doesn't make a lot of sense to me. It is better to try to fix it at the earliest opportunity and give everyone the chance to improve if they can. And if they don't take that chance? Well, nothing speaks more loudly than not bringing back your business.

10

—≡

BEYOND THE BALLS

I was in the kitchen at the pass, waiting for plates to take to the guests in the dining room. One of the chefs was screaming for things to be brought up – 'Ça marche' … this or that. Another of the chefs, a young man, was late in preparing a dish. I looked at him and he glanced up at me, and suddenly his face turned pale.

His eyes looked as if they were bulging from their sockets. His mouth opened, but no words came out. Just a long, low 'Aargh!' He was in excruciating pain. As I went a little closer to the pass, I could see that the older chef was behind him. He was squeezing the young guy's testicles. 'Move your arse fast,' shouted the testicle squeezer. And the young man moved – but not that fast.

All of this was taking place while, in the serene atmosphere of the dining room, the guests clinked glasses, savouring, silver forkful by silver forkful, the restaurant's legendary pig's trotters stuffed with sweetbreads, chicken mousseline and morels, or confit salmon cooked in goose fat, or a perfectly-risen Soufflé aux Pistaches.

Welcome to La Tante Claire, a three-star Michelin, and the summer of 1992. Oh, what a voyage of discovery I was on! (That young chef, by the way, survived, became famous and went on to have children.)

John Major was Prime Minister, Princess Anne was recently divorced, and Alan Shearer had become Britain's most expensive footballer (a £3.6 million transfer from Southampton to Blackburn Rovers). I, meanwhile, had become a chef de rang at La Tante Claire, a magnificent restaurant in Royal Hospital Road, Chelsea, a few minutes' walk from the River Thames. It was extremely fine dining, although the phrase 'fine dining' was not in common use at the time. Needless to say the salary was not up there with Shearer's.

I was here because I wanted to spend a year in a renowned restaurant. That was the advice given to me by Alain Sourzac, my God of a teacher at catering college. One year on the CV was what I needed. It would take balls. But I reckoned I had them.

——◄═

In this profession, most of us know that you should spend at least a year in a job as you work your way to the top. Twelve months is the minimum. You might hate the job and yearn to leave it after two, three or five months. But in a top restaurant you persevere, keep your head down and work hard until you have arrived at the magic 12. A young man came for an interview recently at Galvin at Windows. He was after a job as a waiter. During the course of the interview he was perfectly charming, some might say convincing. Once he had left, we had a chat about him, as you do in my business. I said, 'We'll give him a trial. See what he's like. But we probably won't take him on, though. Let's see, he might surprise us.'

Why not? Because his CV told the story of a man who flitted from one job to another. Two months at one restaurant, three months at another, and five months somewhere else. I was curious enough to give him a trial but his CV strongly suggested that he could not be relied upon. Who is to say that after we had invested our time and energy in him, he would not simply hand in his notice, before we were able to see the fruits of our labour?

I knew how important the magic 12 months were when I left Limoges, crossed the Channel, and came to London in that summer of 1992. At catering college I had taken my exams for my baccalaureate but did not wait for the results before saying farewell to my family in Limoges. 'You can't go, you don't have your exam results,' said my mother. 'You don't know whether you've got it or not.' She wanted me to go to university for a couple of years even though that certainly was not a part of my plans.

As it transpired, I had not only passed the exams but had received the second highest mark achievable. In fact, Monsieur Sourzac's class proved to be an exceptional year, with an all-time record number of students receiving credits.

My exam results were good news and they would be great for my CV, but I would only receive those results two months after I had arrived in England, at which point I was working at La Tante Claire. At that time, La Tante Claire was one of only three restaurants in Britain to have the accolade of a Michelin star. The other two were held by the Roux brothers.

I ended up at Tante Claire through a friend at catering college. His name was Fabrice Julienne, but we called him Julio – not an abbreviation of his surname, but because he was as ridiculously good looking as Julio Iglesias, the debonair Spanish singer. Julio (my friend, rather than the singer) had worked a placement at Tante Claire the previous year. 'It's amazing,' he said. 'You could go there if you want.'

So he made the call, and I sent in my CV and that was how I got a job at this world-renowned restaurant. Life teaches you about the connections that you make and the people that you meet, and you can only form these connections if you go to the right places. *La crème*, as they say, always rises to the top. Apart from the fine education I received at Souillac, the college also instilled in me a champion-like mindset. Thanks to my teachers, I realised I was not at college simply to become a waiter. I was to be the best, to perform as brilliantly as possible and to do something that I enjoyed passionately. My vision was to reach the top, to be la crème. And then to be *la crème de la crème*.

For Frenchmen coming to London there were only a few places that fitted the criteria set by my tutors at catering college. Apart from The Waterside Inn, Le Gavroche and La Tante Claire – all of them with French chef-patrons – there were the restaurants of the five-star hotels: The Savoy, The Connaught and The Lanesborough. However, the face of London's restaurant scene was just beginning to change, with Terence Conran launching huge, buzzy establishments, such as Quaglino's and Le Pont de la Tour. The revolution had begun.

The chef-patron at Tante Claire was Pierre Koffmann, a master in our industry. Big, broad and bearded, he is known as Pierre the Bear. He is a fantastic chef – eccentric and amusing. But it is fair to say that while he was a genius at the stove, and had the most fantastic relationship with food, his interpersonal skills were sometimes not quite as good. I am not the first former employee, and doubt I will be the last, to say that his leadership style was never going to win him any awards for Employer of the Year. He had a fierce temper.

During one service, I was in the kitchen waiting to collect an order, when Pierre the Bear looked at me from the other side of the pass. He walked towards me, put his huge bearded face next to mine – we were almost close enough to kiss – and then he burped right in my face. It was probably the loudest burp I have ever heard. Of course, I had done nothing wrong, this was just the Bear's weird sense of humour. Strangely, I did find it funny, and I burst out laughing.

'It makes you laugh?' said Pierre. I am not sure I was supposed to laugh.

'What do you want me to do?' I said. 'Cry?'

At this, he turned around to get something from the counter, bent down slightly, raised his huge bottom into the air and farted. It was enough to put you off your stuffed pig's trotters. In terms of volume, the fart competed with the burp. Pierre's brigade carried on regardless, as if this behaviour was in no way extraordinary. Because, in this kitchen, it was not. But for all his kitchen antics, Pierre could be shy or socially awkward when away from his kitchen, his territory. Guests would say, 'Oh, is Pierre here? I'd love to say hello.' Poof! He would disappear; he did not like to perform for the public.

—◀≣

Before opening his own restaurant and winning stars, Pierre had arrived in Britain from Gascony in 1970, and had worked for the Roux brothers, first at Le Gavroche and then as head chef at the Waterside Inn. (In fact, many of the top people in London have either worked for Michel and Albert Roux, or worked for someone who worked for the brothers; or for Michel Jnr, or for Michel's son, Alain. So there you have the roots, if you like, of our experience. Roux roots.) Pierre had only come to Britain to watch France play England at rugby, but he ended up staying, to the great delight of Britain's gourmets and connoisseurs.

Even if his own management style was unorthodox, his team really looked after me. The restaurant had employed plenty of French chefs and waiters so they knew the drill for the new arrivals. They helped me to open a bank account, obtain a National Insurance number and they sorted out my accommodation.

Tante Claire was overseen by the restaurant manager, Jean-Pierre, who was in his forties, had a balloon belly and was a delightful man, much adored by the guests. When I asked him how busy we were for lunch, he responded, 'At Tante Claire we are always busy. Always full. No need to ever ask how busy we are.' It was a bit curt, not helpful or friendly to say the least. Still, he had a point. The restaurant was always busy, everything had to be ready on time and all the time. And if I, or anyone else for that matter, ever thought that there could be some downtime or less to do, we were sorely mistaken: downtime simply did not exist.

Before the madness of service, we sat outside on crates and often – a little too often, to be honest – ate spaghetti Bolognese, made not from beef mince but from lamb's hearts, for our staff meal. I read a magazine interview with Tom Kitchin, in which he was asked about the most unusual food he had eaten. 'Duck's testicles in the kitchen at La Tante Claire,' answered Tom. 'Pierre would put them on the hot stove to cook and then feed them to the chefs; a bit of oil, salt and pepper. He'd eat them as well. But I've not eaten them since.' The waiters were spared this 'delicacy'. This was just one part of Pierre's drive to minimise waste of any sort.

He also had a very clever way of recycling the dregs of wine left by the guests. The wine was ridiculously expensive and you may be surprised that not all of it was drunk. The glasses were taken from the table and into the kitchen. There, the contents were emptied into bottles. This wine was then used to make sauces. It meant that if you were wealthy enough to be a regular guest, you could be drinking a particular claret on, say, Monday and then, come lunchtime on Thursday, you could be eating a sauce made with the same claret that had been left in your glass earlier in the week. This was recycling before the word came into common parlance. Of course, the guests did not know what happened to their dregs in this three-star Michelin establishment. Had they done so, they might have been worried about germs.

And it didn't just apply to food. Each chef was assigned just one apron and two chefs cloths every day. This was never enough. When you were mopping up spilt milk, protecting your hands from a hot pan, wiping the sweat off your brow, having just two cloths meant that everything got dirty pretty quickly, and people stashed them anywhere they could think of. As a waiter, luckily I didn't need to worry about dishcloths.

My home was a bedsit in Pimlico, where the weekly rent was £50. For that, I had a small room with a view overlooking a courtyard. I was a five-minute walk from work. The work rota was simple – Monday to Friday on; Saturday and Sunday off. In terms of lifestyle it was great. The Monday-to-Friday set-up eliminated the usual fuss of weekend shifts. This rota was similar to many of the top restaurants. You knew when you started. You did not know when you would finish – but you knew where you stood. Overtime did not really exist in our profession.

Things have since evolved, and for the better, I have to say. Nowadays many restaurants ask their staff to work, for example, 48 hours each week. The staff are also paid for all the hours they work over and above the contractual number of hours. This is right, again, and very good for the industry. As my dad would say, 'Toute peine mérite salaire.' Every little chore deserves payment. That is understandable.

People talk a lot about 'work-life balance': how to manage or balance the time that is spent at work with the time that is spent relaxing and winding down. We are told that we all have to find a way of managing the two. I do not think there is such a thing as a work-life balance. If you want something you have to work for it. All you get from nothing is nothing. And anything that you think will be fantastic will require hard work; a sacrifice has to be made. You cannot be a boxing champion if you go to the pub every day and drink eight pints of beer. 'You can always be what you want to be,' Sugar Ray Leonard said, 'if you are willing to sacrifice and dedicate yourself.' Sacrifice and dedication are the two main ingredients in the recipe for achievement.

You cannot just fulfil a professional ambition without immersing yourself in the job. This is just the way it is; the way success happens. And so there is an innate contradiction in the term 'work-life'. Work is part of life; the two do not have to be separated. I breathe when I work and I breathe when am off. It's all living for me. And I love it.

We are also told that the young people are lazy and not interested in work. This is not true. Indeed, 400 years before the birth of Christ, Socrates was writing about how the younger generation was lazy and did not respect their elders – 'they love chatter in place of exercise'. In my experience, some people are hardworking while others are not, irrespective of their age. This is the same today as it was when I was growing up. The fact is, if you are in any business and want to succeed then at some point you have got to put your head down and do what it takes. And when you have done that, you can take a breather and decide what you do next.

At La Tante Claire, the waiters were known as *la chair à canon* – cannon fodder. Whenever we had finished our jobs in the dining room we had to help the cooks shell peas or prepare the green beans. Good old countryside values! What was not so good was the impenetrable inner circle around Jean-Pierre.

Either you were in or you were out and this led, at times, to an uncomfortable and oppressive atmosphere. Other waiters didn't last more than a week; but I stuck it out for the magic 12 months, learning a lot about England and teamwork along the way.

When I got to the end of that twelfth month, in July 1993, I handed in my notice. I had accomplished that crucial year on my CV and so I was free to move on.

11

THE JOY OF REGULARS

Most people are content to eat out, and take it as it comes, safe in the knowledge that (presumably) someone has taken great care to ensure that they are happy with the menu, the table and the atmosphere. These people do not quibble. Then there are those who know precisely what they want in order to make the experience the most pleasurable for them – to shape the restaurant around their very personal needs and desires. You do not need to be in this business for long to encounter eccentric or unconventional guests. They are the people who visit a restaurant with specific requests or demands. They are set in their gastronomic ways. Others might regard them as 'difficult', but I find them interesting and just as deserving of attention as any other guest. Usually it is a pleasure to look after them, and they will reward you with loyalty as long as you continue to meet their particular needs.

During my time at Tante Claire, London was still home to the era of the ridiculously long lunch and exuberant dinner. 'Charge it to expenses!' was the rallying cry. The Bear's restaurant was very good at indulging guests who had both the time and the money (or large expense accounts) to sit, linger, and enjoy exquisite food and fine wine. And to do so over a period of four, five or even six hours. Some people would arrive for lunch at noon and, come 6pm, they were just finishing the meal, amid the scents of cognac, Comté and Cuban cigar smoke.

There was one particular gentleman, a regular, and at the end of his meal one day I asked him, 'Would you like another coffee, sir?' He ordered espresso. Shortly afterwards I asked if he would like another. 'Yes, please.' This continued until he had drunk five large espressos. I said to my manager, 'This could be dangerous. What about his heart?'

Jean-Pierre looked at me, and said, 'Are you a doctor? If he wants another espresso, just give it to him. Give him as many cups of coffee as he wants. Do as he wishes. It's not for you to judge him or to tell him whether it's good for his health or not.' This was a good lesson and Jean-Pierre was right, of course. The guest was there to enjoy himself, and that he did.

Another gentleman who comes to mind is the director of an extremely profitable company. About once a month, he arrives at Galvin at Windows with a small entourage, any number of a wide variety friends or associates. He is generous and good company, so it is no surprise that he is popular. Once at the table, he never veers from his favourite wines. During the meal he will have a red from Bordeaux, and his meal is incomplete without it finishing like this – he orders a bottle of Château d'Yquem, the finest of the Sauternes … and a banana.

The banana is served, sliced on a dessert plate, just as he likes it. For him, the sweet wine and banana are the perfect pairing. 'Fred, sit down, have a seat,' he will say. 'Join us for a moment.' I do not make excuses. We sit and drink a £400 bottle of wine – no more than a glass for me, mind you – as my host says, 'Try a slice of banana with it.' So you can see how these quirky customs of customers are charming and endearing – and they cannot harm profits.

There is also Mr Arfilly, a lawyer who would come for lunch every Friday at Galvin at Windows. He was a cheerful gourmet. He had his own special menu that catered to his particular taste – which could be summed up as the richer the food, the better – and he drank wines chosen for him by our sommeliers. He knew what he liked and he liked the good stuff.

He loved to eat and drink so much that, with the deepest affection, we referred to him as 'the walking foie gras'. Sometimes he brought a business associate for lunch, by the end of which they were a little wobbly, but good for them! One day Mr Arfilly stood up slowly and then fell over. Bump! Clearly, he was overwhelmed by the sheer joy of the table. We helped him to a comfortable chair in the bar.

I would always join him at his table for a friendly chat. When I told him that I was having trouble with my builders, he stepped in to help. I had paid the builders a substantial deposit, but the work had never been done. 'Of course, you are due the deposit,' said Mr Arfilly. He fired off legal letters, handling the matter and refusing to take a penny for his services. I got my money back from the builder.

Alas, my elderly lawyer friend became seriously unwell with cancer. Did the illness stop him visiting the restaurant on the twenty-eighth floor of the Hilton in Park Lane? Not a bit of it. Nothing, it seemed, could deter the great gourmet from the delights of good food and wine.

He would arrive at the hotel by taxi, and from there he was helped into one of the hotel's wheelchairs. Then he was brought up in the lift, wheeled to his table and helped into his chair so that he could begin his feast, gazing out through the windows across London. During lunch he continued to work, too; if dining alone he would be on his mobile phone, talking business. After lunch, he got back into the wheelchair, went down in the lift to the ground floor, and returned home by taxi.

This ritual continued every Friday for some months until, one day Mr Arfilly arrived and unfortunately there were no wheelchairs available to transport him to his restaurant heaven. He did not ask the cab driver to take him home. Instead, a couple of members of staff helped him walk to the lift, and up he came. At the twenty-eighth floor, he was warmly greeted and helped to his table, where he stayed blissfully for a few hours, relishing lunch with all the usual gusto we had seen so often. Perhaps the Bordeaux was overly potent on that day, but by the time he had finished lunch we felt that the return journey to the taxi would be too much without a wheelchair. As there was not a wheelchair available, we had to improvise. 'Will you please go downstairs to the lobby and bring up a luggage trolley?' I asked a waiter. A few minutes later, he appeared with a very large, gold luggage trolley.

'Do not move an inch,' I said to Mr Arfilly as he sat in his chair.

'I promise you I won't,' he said, and smiled.

While he remained seated, we lifted both the chair and its

occupant and put it on the trolley. Then Mr Arfilly was wheeled to the lift, thence through the ground-floor lobby and to the taxis outside, waving farewell to the staff. He looked like a king on his litter, being carried through the cheering throng.

Shortly afterwards I received a memo from Security, asking me, 'not to put your guests on luggage trolleys'. Mr Arfilly came every week until his illness finally took him to a heaven far higher than the twenty-eighth floor. Even now on Friday lunchtimes I often think of Mr Arfilly and smile.

———⊨

Mr Arfilly was one of those guests who was adamant about what he wanted to eat: anything with butter and cream. There are many others who stick to precisely the same dishes on every regular visit. Remember Madame La Clem, the elderly lady at La Baule, who ate langoustines and mayonnaise for lunch every day? Every restaurant has their special, regular guests.

I know of one restaurant where a regular guest always arrives with his wife, and what follows never changes. He asks for his bread to be extra crispy on its edges, and insists on unsalted butter. He orders one bottle of the usual wine – no more, no less – and a bottle of still water – no more, no less. He always orders for himself and for his wife, and they always have the same dishes from the menu. They begin the meal: deep-fried prawns with chilli sauce for him; deep-fried prawns – with no chilli sauce – for her. To accompany the prawns, and for extra heat, he always orders a side dish of chopped chilli pepper. For mains, they both have fish. Always. Before the main courses arrive, he always asks a waiter, 'Please may I see the menu?

We'd like to order dessert.' This order means they won't have to wait long in between finishing the mains and starting desserts. I do not know if their desserts differ on each visit.

This sort of guest might seem difficult because they are so particular, but in fact they are an asset to the restaurant. They are regulars, and can be counted on to contribute to the financial stability of the restaurant and therefore our wages. To the observer, there is monotony – these guests, it seems, are not adventurous enough to choose a new wine or a different dish from the menu. Yet their predictable ways should never be underestimated because they want precision and if they do not get it, and something goes wrong, the whole machine can crash and cause chaos. Now, of course, that is true of any complaint but with a particular regular, you run the risk that you will lose an important part of your business. And of course, they have always been so clear with you that there isn't really an excuse for messing up.

For instance, I knew a gentleman who would take his wife to a certain restaurant for Sunday lunch every six weeks. She was blind, and he would request a table by the window so that he could describe what was happening to her. Without fail, his order was the same every time – he wanted his beef cooked medium-well, three carrots and four roast potatoes. Now, usually he was served by the same waiter, a friend of mine, who knew and appreciated what he wanted. There was never a problem because the waiter did his utmost to avoid any problems because he feared what could happen and the disruption it might cause.

But one particular Sunday the gentleman and his wife were served by a different waiter. The order was not delivered as instructed. Maybe the beef was underdone, or there were three potatoes and not four. I am not sure. Whatever the case, the guest summoned his favourite waiter and said, in a gentle, polite way, 'I ordered my usual, but I haven't received it as I usually do. It's really not good enough. We are going home.' They left. While the couple did return, my friend was always even more careful to be well prepared. He knew what they liked and so he always ensured that, before they arrived, he had considered all this, and was ready. 'Otherwise,' my friend said to me, 'I would have to spend five minutes at the table fixing the problem.' He was happy to fix the problem but it meant that he could not give his attention to other guests. His mission, therefore, was to be so well organised that there were no problems to fix.

There are guests, too, who take their pets to restaurants. This is Britain, after all. People take their dogs or cats out for lunch or dinner, and feed them morsels from the table. I've seen it! I also know of a restaurant where one of the regulars arrives with a parrot on his shoulder, in the style of the pirate Long John Silver. In the dining room, the colourful bird perches on the back of chair at the table while his owner eats. The restaurant manager does not mind, although the parrot still has a little way to go in terms of table manners. One particular lunchtime, the parrot squawked, flapped its wings and launched itself off the back of the chair. He flew across the room and landed in the middle of another table, where ten guests were enjoying their meal. There the parrot pecked at the bread before his owner grabbed him. Apologies were made, but the episode was laughed off by the table of ten, and the manager told them, 'The bread is on the house.'

12

———€

THE ICON

Le Gavroche is an icon. There are many who would say there is no other restaurant in London quite like it and I am one of them. After I had finished at Tante Claire, I had to – needed to – to work there. In case you have forgotten, la crème rises to the top. Those waiters, and chefs, who work and learn at both La Tante Claire and Le Gavroche? Those are the people who are la crème de la crème.

The role that Le Gavroche (known familiarly as Gavroche or Le Gav) has played in the history of British restaurants cannot be underestimated. The restaurant began life, not in its current home in Mayfair, but several miles away in Chelsea. There, in Lower Sloane Street, close to Sloane Square, it was opened in 1967 by Albert Roux and his younger brother Michel. London had never known anything quite like it. Back in the late 1960s, Britain was still recovering from the Second

World War and restaurants were not top, or anywhere near the top, of anyone's priority list. Today, chefs are obsessed with the quality of produce and ingredients. Back then, there was little regard for produce that came, mostly, from intensive farming. Today, people from all walks of life are drawn to the fun and exhilaration of our profession: rich, poor, upper class, middle class, working class. Back in the 1960s, to be a waiter or a chef was a job for the working classes.

When people went out for lunch or dinner, there was a limited choice of restaurants, let alone good restaurants. Soho had its Italian trattorias. For those with more money in their pocket, The Savoy had its Grill Room. Albert Roux has since described Britain in this period as 'a gastronomic desert', where many British people were often reluctant to try anything new, wanted their beef well done and preferably with Yorkshire pudding. There were rare Brits, however, who were keen gourmets: the elite, who could afford trips abroad and who knew French food. When Albert and Michel opened Gavroche it was an overnight success thanks to these people.

———————

The birth of French gastronomy in Britain was the opening of Le Gavroche. Perhaps the Roux brothers led what we now view as the British food revolution, although the revolution would take almost three decades to fully establish itself. From there, the brothers went on to open one restaurant after another, building a mighty empire, but not one that was outsized or unmanageable.

In time, Michel would oversee The Waterside Inn, beside the

River Thames in Bray, while Albert would remain at Gavroche. In 1982, Gavroche became the first British restaurant to win three Michelin stars. The Waterside Inn followed. There were almighty changes in 1991, four years before my arrival: Albert resigned, handing over the reins, pots, pans and pass to his son, Michel, known as Michel Jnr to avoid confusion with his uncle.

Michel had trained in France with the gastronomic hero Alain Chapel. Now at the helm, Michel would keep the Gavroche classics, much-loved by the regulars – and, after all, why mess with them? But he added his own style and touches, and dishes, of course. He made other changes, which included the dress code. Albert had insisted that gentlemen should wear ties in the restaurant but Michel did away with this rule. As the new Roux at the pass, he was closely scrutinised by the clientele and the critics, and he was devastated when the restaurant lost a star in the Michelin Guide (to this day it still has two stars). Interestingly, business was unaffected by the loss of that star. When news of the demotion spread, curiosity was aroused and more people came to eat. They wanted to try out the restaurant everyone was talking about, and to see for themselves whether it was worthy of two or three stars. As they say, there is no such thing as bad publicity.

Michel Roux Jr ran the kitchen and, of course, these days he is very well known across the world. Front of house was run by Silvano, a name which will probably mean nothing to you, but belongs to one of the most acclaimed ambassadors of hospitality that Britain has ever known. What a master! He would become my mentor and, my God what a privilege it is to have worked with him.

Every good restaurant needs a boss. The customer wants to see that there is someone in charge. Often in bad restaurants, where there is poor management, it can be difficult to work out who the manager actually is. When you arrived at Le Gavroche, you knew that Silvano Giraldin was the boss; I am sure I was not the only person who thought of him as 'Signor Gavroche'.

He had come a long way. He arrived in London in 1971 at the age of 23 when Le Gavroche had been open for four years. Silvano began as a commis waiter, but swiftly worked his way up, climbing the ranks to become maître d'. By 1976 he was general manager of Gavroche. Michel would later describe him as 'an institution'. Silvano was tough, and the story goes that a potent mix of merciless ambition and self-belief got him to where he was. By the time Silvano retired from Le Gavroche in 2008 he was one of the longest-serving restaurant managers in the history of London restaurants and, without question, one of the capital's greatest hosts.

Even when he was not actually present at Gavroche, his spirit was always there; his influence was so immense, it was as if he was always there in the room – the imperceptible guiding hand.

Silvano was an expert charmer, as I observed in awe when I joined the team, starting as a commis chef de rang in January 1995. He greeted the customers, who smiled back and swooned. 'Hello, how are you? How lovely to see you.' All the while, he cast an eagle eye over the dining room, all of its tables, each member staff and every single one of its customers. Hawk-eyed, clever and meticulous, Silvano missed nothing.

He did not serve the customers; he was not there to serve, to wait on the tables. However, if service started to go down because, for instance, we suddenly became too busy, then he would step in, masterfully resolving all problems. It was his mere presence that encouraged most of us to work hard and work well. Silvano was the guardian of the restaurant's standards, and the ultimate line of defence between the customers and potential headaches. With expert foresight and experience, he could, would and did prevent the storm of poor service if it appeared on the horizon and was quickly blowing our way. He would swoop in just before it hit.

He instilled a mantra in all of us: Le Gavroche has to be clean; Gavroche has to be set; Gavroche has to be ready. Ready for anything. This meant, for instance, that we had to know the menu inside out, as well as the ingredients of the dish, and specifically where they were from, just in case anyone asked. There was no space for short cuts. When we were told to do something by Silvano, we did it – no questions, no quibbles. There were no ifs and certainly no buts. If there were two words that could never be spoken they were: 'But Silvano ...'

All this meant that the dining room of Le Gavroche had that special buzz. It was there at every service, without fail. Certainly, there was laughter and animated conversation in the room, as you'd expect at any good restaurant, but those things by themselves do not guarantee the special buzz. There was also this abundance of sheer joyfulness and happy expectation, combined with glorious food and tip-top service. These created a comfort blanket of bonhomie, so wonderful that you could almost touch it. This ambience is rare in restaurants, even in the best ones. Think of the greatest party you have ever been to, and that will give you a sense of Le Gavroche at lunch and dinner. Truly extraordinary. And it still is, to this day!

People did not come to the restaurant to fuel up. Non, non, non! Instead they came to escape normality, to indulge in style and to treat themselves to the pleasures of haute cuisine. Whether they were there for the first time or the hundredth time, from the moment they stepped through the doorway of 43 Upper Brook Street, Mayfair, and walked down the stairs and into the dining room, their faces instantly lit up with a look of genuine delight. They were, quite simply, having a marvellous time!

The room itself exuded cosiness, helped by generous splashes of red and green, colours that are said to encourage appetite: olive green walls and banquettes of the same colour; round tables with white linen, napkins in silver napkin rings, and red-covered chairs. If silence fell at your table, there was always something to observe. There was interesting artwork, including a few paintings of the restaurant's French founders. Vases of flowers and pots of sweet-smelling, colourful orchids were placed here and there. As it was located in a basement, the room lacked natural light. Apart from the ever-glowing candlelight, the wall lighting was dim and low and set the tone: homely, comfortable and romantic. Come the autumn months, the scents of the orchids and expensive perfumes and cigars would mingle with the distinctive, pleasant muskiness of black truffles, freshly gathered from the forests of south-west France, and transported to the little kitchen of Le Gavroche to be sliced and sprinkled over or incorporated into dishes, such as the sublime artichoke mousse. Seemingly, each and every component came together seamlessly, and in a moment married harmoniously so that – voila! – restaurant magic was made in Mayfair, in that basement room.

The customers dressed smartly for the occasion. They had come for an experience, and wanted to look their best for the occasion. They were, after all, not just having a day out in London, but in Mayfair and just off Park Lane, the two priciest squares on the Monopoly board. The waiters and waitresses were also wonderfully turned out in white jackets and black trousers. One particular head waiter was always immaculate. He wore black brogues that were so well polished they gleamed brightly enough to reflect the candlelight. Today – 20 years after I left Le Gavroche – I can still picture those shoes. The shine, the laces, the unscuffed, pointed tips. I was once on the receiving end of one of those shoes...

It was halfway through a dinner service, and I was entering the dining room, coming from the kitchen pass. I was carrying a silver tray full of dishes for happy, cheerful customers. It was not a long walk to the table where the head waiter was busy schmoozing and charming the seated customers. He turned and looked at me and then, with no warning or explanation, he kicked me in the right shin, not a big swing of a kick, but a killer one.

Ouch! A stabbing pain shot from my leg and through my body. It hurt like hell. Somehow he had managed to perform the kick without anyone else noticing. Why didn't they see it? Two reasons: first, he was clearly skilled and knew how to get away with it; second, I suppose that my legs were hidden by the large tray that I was carrying in my hands. If any of the customers did notice, then nothing was said. There were no cries of, 'Hey, did you see that! That waiter just kicked the other waiter!'

Kicking waiters is not common in restaurants. I had not

experienced it before and have not experienced it since. Mind you, I doubt I was the first waiter to be kicked during service, and I will probably not be the last. However, I expect it is fair to say that most of us do not go out for dinner, hoping for a fantastic meal with the added bonus of seeing waiters kick each other in the shins with shiny, pointed brogues.

Okay, so now my shin was hurting. I was standing in the middle of the dining room and holding a heavy tray. Around me were the sounds of laughter and bonhomie, as well as the clink-clink of Champagne flutes and the tap-tap of forks, knives and spoons as customers tucked into the restaurant's classics: Soufflé Suissesse (made with gruyère cheese and cream), the lobster mousse with caviar, Poulet de Bresse en Vessie (chicken from Bresse, poached in a pig's bladder).

Very quickly I started to feel angry: who was he to do this to me? If I had not been holding the tray, I would have hit him there and then. But if I had not been holding the tray then maybe he wouldn't have kicked me. I don't like to dither, I like to get things done. I said to myself, 'Once the food is served, I am going straight back to the kitchen to dump this tray. Then I am going to come back into the dining room and I am going to punch this idiot very, very hard.'

I hobbled as fast as I could out of the dining room into the kitchen. I put down the empty silver tray beside the pass, with the food still on it. Then I marched – as fast as I could with a limp – back into the dining room. My assailant was there, all wide smile, cologne and schmooze. I said his name, and he turned around to face me.

'Yes?' he said.

I could not do it. Not in front of the customers, So I said,

'Oh, nothing …' I returned to the kitchen, picked up another tray of food from beside the pass, and carried it back into the dining room to deliver the dishes to the customers. There was a culture of bullying that had existed in restaurants for decades and continued into the 1990s, when I was at Le Gavroche, and beyond. Staff tended to live with it, put up with it, because it was just that – part of the culture. That was the way of the world, behind the scenes of what we call hospitality. Many restaurants were brutal environments. Much has changed, I am happy to say, with the introduction and development of employment laws, and a change for the better in the way we think, so that the humble employee is protected from physical and verbal abuse. Nowadays, if you were kicked at work by a colleague, there is every chance that member of staff would be given the sack. But back then there was very little to be achieved by complaining.

But I am stubborn and I was young, so yes, I did complain. I went to see Silvano. 'That man,' I said, 'he kicked me. Apart from that, he insulted me. He is very difficult to work and it's completely outrageous. He's out of order and creates so much trouble out of nothing.'

'Fred,' said Silvano, ever the voice of authority and reassurance. 'I know what he is like. But you have to see his good side. Look at how clean Gavroche is, and how good the staff look. In many ways, he is doing a good job. Ignore his words. He is like an old woman. Don't listen to him.'

You might wince at what Silvano said, but on reflection, I had learned an important lesson. In the years to come, I would work with – and take on – people who were not quite up to the job. For one reason or another, they might not be the best waiters or waitresses. However, I always look for their good side. I focus on what they are capable of doing, as well as working on their faults. I want to ensure that they can add value and deliver our vision to our guests. But I will never stand for abusive behaviour. If you do it, you are out, no matter who you are. Full stop.

There was never a second kick, I am extremely pleased to say. Waiters should not have to wear shin pads to work!

14

THE CUSTOMER IS KING
(OR QUEEN)

At Le Gavroche, and under the tutelage of Silvano, I learned so much. Above all, he taught me that that the customer is king, which he genuinely believed that to be the case. There was no shred of doubt in his mind about this. I still maintain this same rule. The customer must be happy, therefore it is our task to help put the customer in the best of moods, no matter what it takes. Most of the time, of course, this is covered by following the rules of good service in a restaurant. But sometimes, things are far more precarious than that.

It was New Year's Eve at Galvin at Windows, one of our busiest nights of the year. Soon it would be midnight, with the pop, pop, pop of Champagne corks, and the guests tipsily breaking into a chorus of, 'Should auld acquaintance be forgot. And never brought to mind …'

A certain Russian gentleman was about to walk into my life,

and it seems to me still that he was sent to test me to the limit on the idea that customer is king. The lift arrived on the twenty-eighth floor of the London Hilton on Park Lane, the doors opened, and this man and his entourage emerged. He was a big guy, in his forties, and he was probably the only person who was not smiling. That was the first problem. Normally, guests arrive smiling, excited to be there and amazed by the view. It is rare that they aren't, and it is never good.

He had booked a table. As we stood at reception, he pointed to a table near the window, and said, 'We'd like to sit there.' Now, of course, it was New Year's Eve so we were fully booked, and that particular table near the window was booked for 11 people who were about to arrive. The table I had reserved for the Russian was in the centre of the room, perfectly set up for him and his five guests. That night, to ensure smooth service on such a busy and special evening, we were seating guests in alternate stations, according to the size of the party, some near the windows and some not. Moving things around would not have been possible without disrupting all our careful work.

I told him as much, and of course, he was unhappy. This situation could annoy anyone, but it took only a minute or two for him to become rude. I tried explaining exactly how the table plan worked, giving more detail than I usually would to try and calm him down. Throughout the explanation, I was holding the reservation list. He snatched the piece of paper from my hand and interrupted me: 'I don't care about your booking policy.'

With hindsight, I believe that I would have been totally justified in saying to him 'You know what? I am not taking any more nonsense, Sir. You don't have to be rude. I have explained what is happening, and I want to make amends, even though I haven't done anything. But this is going too far.'

Indeed, few would have blamed me for telling him to get lost. But I did not say any of that or even consider saying it, because the customer is king, even customers like this. 'Sir, please don't be upset,' I said. 'Just enjoy New Year's Eve. Please … I understand you don't have the table you want and I am sorry about that. There's nothing I can do about the table. As you can see, we are fully booked. But I do want you to be happy.' I added, 'Look, it is New Year's Eve, I want you to be happy. The whole thing is on me.'

But he was adamant. 'It's not about money. I have come here, to Galvin at Windows to see the fireworks, and I expect that table …' He pointed to the one by the window; the one where eleven people were now seated and enjoying their New Year's Eve. 'I'll get you sacked,' he said to me. I looked around. Everyone else seemed to be having an extremely good time.

'I'll buy the hotel and sack you.'

I tried reasoning with logic. 'Sir, look – that is a table for eleven … So I couldn't give you that table … You and your friends will have to go to that table. The table in the centre, for six, will provide a much more pleasant setting for your evening … This is about you being happy and we will do what we can to make you happy.' I did not want him to think that I was ignorant and did not know how to do my job, or that I did not care about his frustration and unhappiness. I tried my hardest to show that I understood what he was saying and wanted to resolve the problem.

This discussion went on for what seemed like ages. Eventually, the gentleman and his guests took the table in the centre of the room. It did not matter to me if he was Russia's wealthiest man, or a man of modest means. As I said to him, and I must emphasise to you now, it was not a question of money. I did not care about how much he had in the bank or how much he would spend with us during that evening. I wanted to make him smile. For many people in the hospitality industry, the great joy of this job is putting a smile on the customer's face – even if, at times, this seems like an impossible task.

That was not the end of it. Next, I asked one of the waitresses to take over a bottle of Dom Perignon, on the house. Not the house champagne, which would be my usual choice in this situation but Dom Perignon, at £300 a bottle. I wanted to make clear to him that I was going over and above what others might have done, and I understood the sort of man he was.

But did this work? No. From his seat, he glared at me across the room as I looked after other customers by the window. Then he raised his hand in the air, giving me a two-fingered salute. How charming. I tried to read his actions, and took them to mean that he was saying, 'One bottle of Dom Perignon? there are six of us!'

So I sent a second bottle of Dom Perignon to the table. Another £300! Still he seemed dissatisfied, giving me more stern looks, but I saw something in his eyes that seemed to suggest that perhaps I had finally won him over with my kindness and attention. I gave myself a moment to consider the situation. I broke it down as follows: 1. It is New Year's Eve; 2. The guests expects something special when they come to Windows at Galvin; 3. The guests expect a window table; 4. He does not feel like we have made him feel special, because he expected a window table; 5. The customer is king. Also,

I thought, why should I judge him when I know that I can definitely be a tricky customer when I go to restaurants and often ask for a better table.

I went to the table, held out my arms out as if I was Jesus on the cross, and said to him, 'What do you want me to do? Do you want to crucify me? Because Sir, look, I've done everything I can. I've really tried to make you feel good. I've given you some great champagne. I'm as genuine as it comes. I really want you to have a good time, Sir.'

Another general manager may well have told him to get lost, to go somewhere else. That manager would have ruined the gentleman's evening – even more – and lost a customer for life. Or I could have completely ignored the man and, again, made an enemy for life.

Instead, I took it on the chin. All my years of experience in the world of restaurants, I like to think, have taught me how to determine the path to avoid and the one to take. I said to myself, 'You know what? I'm losing this evening, but it's not about losing. I am on the back foot but I want this gentleman to be happy.' It was as simple as that. I didn't know what had happened in his life, or on that day. There could have been an explanation for his behaviour, though not one that I was privy to.

I was determined to give the Russian something – more than champagne, something that no one else in the room would be getting. So we took the Russian and his guests onto the restaurant's balcony, where they watched the fireworks going off all over London. We gave to them far more than we gave to others, and when they finally left us at 3am, the previously furious Russian was in extremely high spirits. Indeed, he even left a large tip for the staff – but this story is not about money. This story is more about how he was treated like a king – the type of king he would recognise – and as a result his attitude changed. One moment he had wanted to sack me and the rest of the staff, but by the end he was pleased, delighted even, and we were all invited to go on a tour of Moscow with him and stay in his dacha for the weekend! Talk about a turn around.

Since then, the Russian gentleman has returned many times to eat, drink and be merry. He sends a lot of people to the restaurant, recommending us as a must-visit place when in London. Meanwhile, I tell this story to my staff because it illustrates the need – no matter what your age or experience – to treat the customer as king, and to reason and think sensibly.

London is one of the best cities to observe the dining customs and habits of guests from around the world as its restaurants are always filled with a cosmopolitan and eclectic range of people. I realise I am making generalisations but this is based on over 25 years of experience.

As my previous story illustrates, Russian guests – although by all means not all of them – can be dismissive towards the restaurant's staff, which, for some, might be regarded as rudeness – after all, it very easy to say 'Please' and 'Thank you'. But I think it comes down to the language barrier and a difference in culture. They can appear stern and aloof and it is not easy to get beyond this.

The Japanese like to eat early, which is is great because they arrive for dinner at 6pm and by 8pm they are gone. A restaurateur's dream. Then you can reset the table, and it is ready for more guests. Brilliant!

Americans fall broadly into two genres. There are the

American tourists who, like the Japanese, eat early and drink Coca-Cola with their meal. Then there are the discerning Americans who can be either: a. boring bankers; or, b. fun, interesting, well-travelled people that you can have a conversation with, just as you can with the Danes who are extremely polite and love food and wine of the highest quality.

Wealthy Middle Eastern guests do not come to expensive restaurants as 'walk-ins' or passing trade. Instead, they – or rather their staff – go to some trouble before the booking is even made. First, the staff come in to check out the restaurant. They might come in once, or twice, or even three times. It can be touch and go. Will they, won't they make a reservation? Then, if the table ends up being booked, a second table is also booked for the same time – this second table is for the guest's bodyguards.

I have worked in restaurants where Middle Eastern guests, who are my regulars, have asked, 'May I have my tea, please.' This is code between you and the particular guest. A teapot is then taken to their table. To everyone else, the guest appears to be drinking tea. For religious reasons, he cannot drink alcohol, but what nobody knows is that the teapot contains vodka or gin.

French guests are 50:50 just like the national rugby team – you never know what you are going to get! Either they enjoy what they eat and drink and the whole experience, or they moan about the food or about what is going on in France. Meanwhile, if you are a restaurateur, and are running a promotion or an offer, then you know the Chinese will definitely be there. They are seriously savvy and always looking for deals.

In London restaurants, the British guests are made up of

business people (mostly from London) or people from the Home Counties who have taken a day off work to have a long lunch or dinner in town. Of those, some of them regard it as a treat and there are others who eat out frequently, often in exceptional restaurants, and they are more judicious. They are connoisseurs who really do know what they are talking about.

As an example, a few days ago we held a wine tasting as part of the process to organise an exclusive private party and one of the guests whom I know very well knew the wines inside out. She knew the grapes, the wine makers and where the wines were produced. I said to the sommelier, 'You see, guests nowadays know the wine better than us.' The lady was within earshot.

You might feel this was a little harsh, but sometimes a 22-year-old sommelier can have a false idea of what he does. It is both necessary and very productive for him to hear the truth, which is that people take a keen interest in food and wines and might know just as much, if not more, than the sommelier. The bottom line is that the sommelier must not assume that the guest's knowledge is not as vast as his own. So make sure you know your stuff and don't even think about winging it!

Often in this business we see customers who arrive at the restaurant and they are in a bad mood, for one reason or another – indeed, there are some people who will never ever be happy, and it is very important, as a waiter to recognise these people, because otherwise they will drive you mad. For instance, I have a friend who was a waitress in a hotel in the British countryside. There was an elderly lady resident who lived in the hotel, and she was a nightmare. At every meal she complained about something, if not everything. There was nothing they could do right. The lady's incessant whinging was extremely stressful for the waiting staff, as they and the chefs were trying their best to please her, and no one else complained. My friend, however, thought, I will not give up – I am going to make her happy and I am going to make her smile.

So the next morning my friend set out to ensure that every component of the lady's breakfast was perfect, and that every part of service was faultless. The lady ordered a full English breakfast, which was served with toast. It looked delicious. It was well cooked and nice and hot. The accompanying slices of toast were perfect, and hot. There was nothing to complain about. But when the waitress went to the table – hoping for a 'Thank you' – the lady waved a silver knife towards the butter 'And how do you expect me to slice that? It's rock hard!' Oh dear. Sometimes you are trying to put a smile on the face of someone who really does not want to smile. We have all experienced it, whether we are waiters or not.

The other day I was at my gym, in the middle of the boxing ring and I was on the receiving end: one punch after another. The lights were going on and off inside my head with every blow. I was thinking, 'Jeez! What the hell is coming next?' I needed to put my guard back up. I got moving again, trying to be lucid. I knew I had to keep moving – if I was up against the ropes there would be more punishment to come. It was the same with the Russian gentleman on New Year's Eve. That time I was up against the ropes. I needed to move, to act straight away, and I had to forget about my pride. The strategy worked – I lived to fight another day.

In fact, I like the Russian gentleman. We are now friends. He emails me every so often, asking – very politely – if I can get him tables in other restaurants. 'Fred, I would like a table at Le Gavroche. Please can you help me out?' So I email Michel, and fix it up. 'I want a table at Hakkasan. Please can you help me out? I want a table at …' I have gone from the general manager he hated on that New Year's Eve, to a friend he depends upon.

One day he came into the restaurant. It was about 8.30pm. He said, 'I am sorry, Fred. I'm late. I was supposed to come at eight.' Then he handed me a gift. 'I brought this special bottle of vodka for you from Russia. I wanted to give it to you because I still can't forget how you made me feel when I came with my family for New Year's Eve. I just wanted to say thank you because I am sorry…'

I stopped him. 'Please, please. There is no need for apologies.' Inwardly, I felt like I was being handed an award for customer service, rather than a bottle of vodka. He was with his wife that evening, and before he left we talked about what happened on New Year's Eve.

He is a man who trades in precious metals, and he said, 'Look, if somebody calls me and they want a truckload of metals, and then the next day they call again, this time to say they don't want the truck … Well, what do I do? Tell them to get lost? I can't do that because if I tell everyone to get lost then where will that leave me tomorrow?' He paused, reflecting on the analogy. 'You see, I understand what you did because this is what I have to deal with. I thought that was unbelievable, the way you handled things. Thank you.'

So I finally got to see the episode from his perspective, and he got to show me that he had seen it from mine. We had to walk in each other's shoes in order to reach an understanding.

Psychology is an essential part of this business, any business – including sport. In boxing, for instance, when you're in the ring, one minute your confidence is down, the next minute it is up. However, the battle of minds with my Russian friend did not end with a loser – we were both winners. The values that I showed to him were similar to those he showed to his own customers. We met in the middle because we realised that we were both genuine. All of this was underpinned with my firm belief that the customer is king. Remove this notion from the theory of hospitality, and the whole idea falls down.

15

UNAMUSING-BOUCHES

Le Gavroche had a staff set-up that could be described as 'upstairs-downstairs'. This was invisible to the guests of course, but it shaped the way we worked and taught me some valuable lessons. There were the masters upstairs and then there were the servants downstairs, the lowly minions. I was one of the latter. The experienced 'old hands' on staff were very firmly upstairs. Everyone downstairs, of course, wanted to work their way up those invisible stairs.

The downstairs minions ate in the staff changing room. It was a hurried meal. What is more, some 'downstairs' commis (including me) also had to prepare a table in the dining room where the 'upstairs' crowd would eat their staff meal. The seniors ate before service, and they ate with hearty appetites and in some splendour in that beautiful dining room that would soon be filled with customers paying a pretty penny for the privilege. There were usually the same faces at every meal. Michel Roux was there of course, with one or two of his right-hand men from the kitchen. Then there was Silvano. He would bring his assistant to the table, as well as the head sommelier and a head waiter.

As they chatted merrily, we served them beautiful dishes prepared by the kitchen, and presented in the lovely copper pans that are well known to Gavroche regulars. Good wine was poured; there was no skimping. Magnificent cheeses were carried to their table, with biscuits, grapes and celery. What a civilised way to savour that last meal before engaging in the excitement of service. They were guests in their own restaurant, receiving great service – and no bill at the end. As they ate, the rest of us – the riff-raff – watched from corners of the room, as we continued to set up our stations. When they had finished the meal, they left the table or sat and drank a coffee. We would clear the table, and shortly afterwards service would start, as the first guests arrived. Silvano was like the general who feasts well before he leads his troops into battle.

This set-up never bothered me. In fact all I wanted to do was work my way up so I could one day eat upstairs too. I warmed to Michel as soon as I met him. He is a frank, kind and honest man, and by his own admission he has never been as unhealthy as he was in those first few years when he took over from his dad. He suffered from severe migraines, was smoking a packet or two of cigarettes a day and then would have a drink when he got home: the typical chef's diet of cigarettes, booze and lack of sleep. These days, he no longer smokes and is hooked on running marathons. Michel was always able to joke with me. If he told me off then he was right to do so, and five minutes later the matter was dropped, and we started afresh. He is a good man.

Although Albert Roux had handed over (correction, sold) Gavroche to Michel, his father's presence was still palpable in the restaurant. Indeed, he was often visible as he was a frequent guest in the dining room.

Albert owned a large house with extensive grounds in the English countryside, where he kept livestock, a large lake filled with carp where he liked to fish, and, of course, a substantial wine cellar. Every Christmas Albert hosted parties at his country residence, and once I was asked to go along to look after the service. I arrived with plenty of time to set up for the meal, and was greeted by Albert and his beloved dogs. The kitchen was huge, with a tiled floor, a massive Aga range cooker, and a gargantuan wooden table in the centre of the room.

As I commented on the size of the kitchen, Albert said, 'Are you hungry, Fred?'

'Hungry? I'm starving. I've missed breakfast.'

'Take a seat.' He ushered me to a seat at the head of the empty table. 'This is for you.' He gave me a linen napkin. 'And these ...' He placed a knife and fork in front of me. 'And, of course, a glass of orange juice ...' The glass was placed before me, and coffee came a moment later. And then he said, 'I am going to cook you something.'

He lifted two eggs from a bowl, and nodded towards the garden through the window. 'Eggs from my chickens.' He broke the eggs into a frying pan and, on the gentlest heat, he fried the eggs in butter. He served them with bread 'soldiers' that were well-buttered because, with Albert, there is always butter.

The white of the eggs was perfectly round and unblemished. The yolk was yellow-orange and, when pierced with a soldier, did not disappoint. It is said that you can tell how good a chef is by how well he can cook eggs. Just two eggs, but laid a few hours earlier and fried by a master. Delicious!

The guests at the party were due to go hunting in the morning and afternoon. They would return for to shower, and then have aperitifs. They included a number of *les grand chefs*, from both sides of the Channel. Silvano was a guest, *bien sûr*, and I was there to look after everyone. Among those I served was the great Paul Bocuse, an undisputed hero of gastronomy, and one of the founders of nouvelle cuisine. He was in his early seventies, utterly charming and asked me lots of questions about myself. He also had an Opinel knife. 'My dad has an Opinel knife,' I said to him. 'He loves it.' To which Bocuse said, 'I tell you what, I'll send you one.' Bocuse is a god in France and around the world, and I felt honoured to speak with him. He was so genuinely interested in me, that I felt humbled and proud. His lesson in attentiveness has stayed with me ever since. Albert cooked for his guests, and they ate Irish stew, as hearty as can be. No fluff, no flim-flam, no flowers, nothing chichi. Just proper Irish stew – in the Roux style – for 20 of them, washed down with fabulous red wine from Albert's incredible cellar. 'Albert,' said Bocuse, from the other end of the enormous table, 'that is cooking!'

The following spring I received a package from Lyon. Paul Bocuse had not sent me a knife, but he had remembered me and sent a tie embossed with his name. It was as appetisingly yellow as Albert's egg yolk. I treasured the garment and wore it for several years, until it became a little too frayed to be seen in public.

By way of contrast, I had a strained relationship with one of Silvano's head waiters, who had a habit of luring me and many other staff into unnecessary arguments. For instance, he would tell me to do things that I had already done. He would say, 'Do it.'

I would say, 'I've done it …'

'No, you haven't.'

'Yes, I have.'

'No, you haven't.'

'Yes, I have.'

And so it went on and on, the two of us sounding like bickering five-year-olds.

The kitchen brigade included a bully, a huge Englishman who looked 40 but was barely 20, and who was a terrible cook. He had spent about two years in the kitchen at Gavroche, but was confined to making amuse-bouches, those dainty, bite-sized dishes that come to the table at the beginning of a meal as a gift from the chef.

Although he was incompetent, he acted as if he was the head chef. The only thing he excelled at was bullying. Whenever I went into the kitchen to collect the amuse-bouches I was greeted by a torrent of his angry abuse, delivered through gritted teeth. 'You see the amuse-bouches. Yes? You understand. Yes? The amuse-bouches. Yes? You've got to carry them like this. Yes? You dumb French …' Add four-letter words as you wish, and plenty of them. His abuse and rudeness was delivered in front of senior members of staff, and I never understood why no one put him in his place. If someone did that in our kitchen today, they would not dare do it again or they would be out of a job, and if I witnessed it, they would be sacked on the spot.

One day the bully gave up on words, and resorted to violence, though not against me. We were in the staff changing room with Nicolas, a young waiter from the Parisian suburbs who talked and behaved as if he was a Paris gangster, in spite of being just a kid. The bully grabbed Nicolas by the throat and pinned him up against a wall, lifting him up about half a metre off the ground as he did so. As the waiter gasped for breath, the bully said, 'Yeah! What you gonna do?' That kind of episode made the day unpredictable. In the mornings I would leave home knowing I was going into work, but what on Earth was going happen?

Mostly, I did the 'closing' shift that began at two o'clock in the afternoon and finished in the early hours of the following morning, when the final guests had finished dinner and left the restaurant. I would 'close' lunch service and set up the restaurant for the evening: organise the service station, set the tables, hoover the floor and clean the toilets – until they gleamed. I would arrange the cheeseboard, so it was stunning and ready for evening service, with the cheese just at room temperature, not too chilled. Keen and eager, I was always ready, all the jobs done, by 6pm, when it was time for the staff meal. At 6.30, we would finish eating. At 7pm, service began. In the early hours of the following morning, I would 'close' dinner service. I can remember those nights of standing to attention, waiting for the final table to finish – it could be 12.30 or 1am. Apart from the people on that table, there is you, the head waiter and the cashier. None of you know when that table will finish. Lord Something-or-other would be sitting there, enjoying his brandy and smoking his cigar, with his beautiful 'niece' sitting next to him. You cannot do any of the back-of-house jobs, such as counting the linen, you just have stand to attention and wait, not too close to the table, but close enough to notice if the guests would like something else. You do not want to make them feel like they should leave. Gavroche is like a private club. If people want to stay until 2am, they stay until 2am. They are not concerned about time, but to you, the young waiter, every minute seems like an hour. And you have no idea when it will end. And just as the guest raises his hand and you think the bill might be required, he says, 'Another brandy, please.'

'Of course, Sir.'

Every night, I would have prepared my station with plenty of time to spare. However, I had no spare time because I would then have to help other waiters prepare their stations, as they were frequently late. Irritatingly, I found myself doing the work of half of the team because they were not as conscientious or as fast as I was. How was it that I had found the time, but they had not? It infuriated me.

This irritation and frustration was compounded by the fact that I was not congratulated for my efforts, and the others were not reprimanded for being sloppy or late. The way I see it, if a job is to be done, then do it well. It is one thing when people make a mistake, we all do, but if the same mistake is made time and time again, then it is no longer a mistake. It becomes negligence and is unforgiveable. Waiters who pitched up late were being negligent. Even thinking back it makes me feel exasperated. Because they did not take pride in their preparation it meant, to me, that they did not care about the guests. They were not anticipating their needs.

One day Silvano and I had a conversation about a few other members of the team. 'Silvano,' I said, 'I'm pulling my weight and sometimes I feel like I'm pulling their weight, too.' He smiled and then said, 'You know, it is better to have bad staff than no staff at all.' When I was older and was responsible for taking on my own staff, I recalled Silvano's words of advice. He was right. As I have said before, you always need people around you; they will be able to do at least one thing well, and you can teach them how to get better.

Once, I was serving at the guéridon, taking me back to my Monte Carlo days. On this particular occasion, Silvano was carving the duck. As his junior, my role was to serve the French beans. Suddenly there was a slip. The pan of beans fell onto the carpet. That was a mistake. At that moment, I was petrified. 'Oh my God, he's going to kill me.' But Silvano said, 'Don't worry, Fred. Go quickly and get another pan of French beans from the kitchen.' I did as he said, carried on the service, cleaned up the dreaded beans, and that was that. I was thrilled that I was not shouted at, and I never did it again. On that occasion, I did not perform to the best of my ability, but operating a guéridon takes two people and Silvano had to work with what I was offering him.

In fact, I did not see Silvano lose his temper with a member of staff very often. I saw it happen once with a guest, the only exception to his rule that the customer is king – or queen, as you will see from this particular story.

On this occasion an American couple arrived for lunch, but from the moment they sat down, the lady complained. She complained incessantly and about everything – the table, her chair, the lighting, the temperature of the water and the wine.

Nothing could make her happy, and Silvano was becoming irritated. As a starter, she ordered gazpacho, a Spanish tomato soup, which is served chilled. The bowl was placed in front of her and she began to sip. But not for long. She beckoned Silvano. 'This is disgusting. It's Heinz tomato soup,' she said.

'Madame, that is not Heinz tomato soup. We do not serve Heinz tomato soup at Le Gavroche.' Around him, the rest of us continued to serve, but I can assure you we were hanging on every word. Silvano's face was turning red with rage.

The lady tried to argue back, 'I'm telling you, it's Heinz tomato …'

At which point, he interrupted. 'Madame, I would like you and your husband to leave now. There is no bill to pay. Please leave immediately.' He pulled the table away from them and towards him, gesturing for the couple to stand. 'If you don't leave now, I will get the boys to throw you out.' By boys, I think he meant us. 'We don't want you here.' The American couple left, no main course, no bill and no need for the boys to chuck them out. The woman was incredibly rude and Silvano had been pushed too far – but perhaps he also knew that she would never be pleased. There is nothing you can do with someone whose palate thinks that fresh, beautifully seasoned gazpacho is the same as stuff that comes in a can and costs less than £1. I never saw him behave like that again.

He was as kind as could be when he met my parents. They had left their home in Limoges and come to visit me for a few days in London. While they were in town, they dressed up smartly and came for lunch at Gavroche. They could not fail to notice the Hollywood movie star in the room, by which I mean Silvano, such was his charisma. Dapper and impeccably charming, he went to their table with his huge smile and embarked on a long, friendly chat, giving them his undivided attention. As customers, they were, in his eyes, not Monsieur and Madame Sirieix, they were the King and Queen. And that is how he made them feel. Later on, when they excitedly discussed their meal, they spoke of how much they had enjoyed the food. 'Mais,' said my mother – and I knew Silvano was about to be mentioned – 'Silvano ... ah, il est très, très beau.' He is very, very beautiful.

———

One day I asked the very, very beautiful Silvano about a promotion. 'Okay, all right,' he said. 'You can be assistant room service manager at 47.' The dining room of Le Gavroche is in the basement, and the rest of 47 Park Street is a hotel, both private and exclusive. The two properties are separated by a single door. At some point in the past, there had been a neat arrangement whereby Le Gavroche ran the hotel's basement kitchen, and oversaw room service in the building. Gavroche also took rooms, including legendary suite number 36, which were used as private dining rooms. That particular suite also had a lounge, kitchen and bathroom.

My new job as assistant room service manager was essentially a waiter's promotion – I had some new responsibilities, but really I was a glorified waiter. But on the day I arrived, the manager left and suddenly I had a few more responsibilities. Silvano said to me, 'You'll have a month to learn the ropes from Giacomo, and then you'll have three months as acting manager. If things go smoothly, then you'll keep the job. If not, you'll be back as a waiter at Gavroche.'

Now I just had to learn the ins and out of the job. The departing manager was very blasé and cocky but I was an attentive student. I listened, asked questions and carried a small notebook with me at all times, so that I could make notes as Giacomo conveyed the information. This little book became my saviour when Giacomo left. I've kept a notebook ever since, and would recommend doing the same.

I suppose I was a bit like a head butler. The team for 47 comprised six waiters, an assistant manager, a manager and two chefs. As manager, I was responsible for room service in the suites, the hotel's staff canteen and any outside events. I had really been flung in at the deep end. I had neither management experience nor any real knowledge of how room service worked. I was used to the hum of the dining room, not the hush of the private suite. On top of this, I had no guidance – there was no one to advise me, to help me towards shallower waters. Silvano was not there at my side to say, 'Okay Fred, what's happening? What's the situation?'

I had many sleepless nights because of the stress, learning on my feet how to get the most and the best out of my young team. Gradually, we learned how to work together, deliver great service and most importantly to enjoy it. I remember a conversation with Silvano three months into the job, at the end of my probation period. He was happy the department was running smoothly, and so I'd passed probation. The job was mine. Then he asked, 'How much do you want?'

I replied, 'How about £1,000 net?'

'Agreed!' said Silvano. To this day, I think I definitely should have asked for more. Silvano must have been rubbing his hands together, delighted with the good deal, but it was just another lesson that working for Silvano taught me.

Working in room service meant there were some moments of real hilarity. One day a waiter told me there had been an accident during delivery of breakfast to one of the suites. I went up to the suite to take a look: the table had overturned and the breakfast was on the floor. Standing beside it was a couple, a man and woman, in dressing gowns. They looked very sheepish. The woman said, 'We just put the breakfast on the table and it collapsed.' That seemed highly improbable: it was far more likely was that they had had tried to have sex on the table and this is what we all agreed, especially the general manager, who had seen it all before.

Throughout the year there were parties in suite 36, and at Christmas time there were even more, for greater numbers of people, and we would use more suites in order to accommodate the events. Imagine being the host, and having your own exclusive dining room in a beautiful home, but with no need to cook or serve the food. That was the luxury of the suites, most notably 36. Everything was done for you, the host, although at some considerable cost, *naturellement*.

Thirty-six could be booked for groups of guests, from eight to twenty covers, depending on the host's bank balance and his or her generosity. However, the sort of people who hired the suite had no financial concerns whatsoever. They were not the type to scan the prices on a menu or a wine list. At the end of lunch or dinner for, say, 12 or 14 people, the host would pick up a bill of perhaps £4,000–5,000 – quite a substantial sum today, let alone in 1994 and 1995.

Within the suite the small kitchen was used for storing the

fine wines, as well as doing the last-minute food prep and plating up. The food was cooked in the kitchens at Gavroche, and carried by waiters and kitchen staff into 47 and then, via the hotel lift, up to 36. The suite's lounge was used as a reception room, where guests could have an aperitif before heading into the cosy dining room.

At the door of the suite, I greeted guests at they arrived, took their coats and was as polite and affable as can be: I was the 'face' of Gavroche, the brand ambassador, giving them a private glimpse into the world. The usual Gavroche rule applied – give them whatever they want. As each event unfolded, I would check with the host that it was running the way that she or he wanted. 'Please let me know if you would like the service to be more discreet. Would you prefer more privacy?' These, of course, were significant issues. A private dining room, of course, feels more intimate than the dining room of a restaurant, and therefore the waiter's presence is magnified and you have to be hyper-aware.

Beautiful food was served; glorious wines were uncorked. In those days you could smoke wherever you wanted, and people did. At the end of the meal I would carry in a gleaming antique mahogany box and open it to offer expensive Cuban cigars. Using the beautiful house silver cigar cutter, I clipped the ends of the cigars and lit them for the guests. Soon the suite would be full of the extravagant and exotic aromas of Montecristo, Romeo y Julieta, Cohiba or the peppery Bolivar. One day, I realised that I had lost the silver cigar cutter.

'Oh, Fred,' said Silvano 'where has it gone?'

'I don't know where it is,' I said. 'I just don't know where it is.'

'But you know how special and expensive it is. We need to

find it…' He talked incessantly about the cutter until eventually I said, 'Look, Silvano, if you want, I will pay for a new cutter…' I offered him £50 – a lot of money back then – and he took it! I thought to myself, 'Eh? The bastard. That wasn't supposed to happen.' Meanwhile, Silvano was thinking, 'You know what, buddy, you're right. I'll take the money, and you won't lose a cigar cutter ever again.' The cutter was replaced and I guarded it as if it were my own.

Although Silvano was not managing 36 day-to-day, nothing passed him by. One day he appeared in the corridors out of the blue, bellowing my name, and calling me an imbecile. I was in trouble because I had ordered more bin bags than were necessary. This might seem trivial, but every small amount of money affects the profits, and waste is unacceptable in this business – at all levels. I let him yell at me, and then off he marched. His mood was so extreme that it began to affect my subconscious. He even appeared in my dreams, but then I suppose I had nothing else to dream about – my life, day in, day out, was about keeping him happy, even if I was in the relative sanctuary of 47.

I had one recurring dream in which Silvano's head was on a long, thick, serpent-like neck (Silvano did have a large neck) that would stretch towards me, his face coming closer to mine as he yelled, 'Fred! Fred! Frrr-R-E-D!' I tell you, I would wake up drenched in sweat. In reality, I had nothing to fear. Before my arrival at 47, there had been complaints about the way the department was run, but within three months I had improved the situation. Everyone was happy, or rather, they were happy – however, my life was not my own there, and the time had come to take another path.

16

———⋐

LES TRÈS IMPORTANTS

Service is a finely balanced art and there's a very narrow margin of error. I call this the domino effect: if a single domino falls, the entire formation will follow, and in the same way a single mishap can lead to catastrophe in the middle of service.

Most of the time the tumbling dominoes are limited to one table: something goes wrong, and then there is another problem, and another … However, once the first domino has fallen, it is the job of a skilled and experienced manager and their team to spot it straight away and do what they can to prevent any more dominoes following, taking the whole table from a great experience to a bad one.

This doesn't just happen at the table. The first domino might fall at reception. Let's say the guest has booked a table but their reservation cannot be found. This is careless and embarrassing, yes, but it happens even in the best restaurants. There's still a chance the rest of the dominoes with remain upright, if you are careful and luck is on your side. Next, you take the guests to their table. To restore their goodwill, you serve each of them a complimentary glass of Champagne ... but you are tired, it has been a long day and, as you pour the champagne, some is spilled, on the tablecloth probably, but perhaps – *quelle horreur!* – on a guest. Down goes the second domino.

Then you take the order. That seems to go well, and yet somehow you did not know that the kitchen has run out of the special, which three of the table decided to order after you explained it so perfectly. You only learn that the special is off when you reach the kitchen with the order and so now you have to return to the table and tell three of the guests that the dish he or she really wanted is no longer on the menu. 'I am terribly sorry Madame, but we have just served our last salmon.' The third domino has just toppled.

Can it get any worse? It can and it will. A guest at this particular table had requested that their lamb be cooked pink. Once served, you ask if everything is all right. 'I asked for pink, this lamb is overdone.' There you have the fourth – and you pray, final – domino. Your prayers, alas, are not answered. If you have ever watched a domino race, then you will know they never stop at four. The coffee is served, but it is served late – domino number five. Quick! Check the cloakroom to make sure another guest has not wandered off, wearing the domino guest's overcoat, the final straw.

The domino effect is the sod's law of the dining room. When they begin to go you are right to fear that every possible problem at every possible stage is heading your way. Watch out for it. Be on your guard. When that first domino falls, it needs to be instantly recognised and checked to stop the other dominoes toppling.

The domino effect should never happen to any guest, but particularly not to a VIP. Perhaps this seems obvious, but every decent restaurant has its Very Important People, who matter for business more than anyone else. Now, these people might be members of the Royal Family, Hollywood movie stars, singers or TV celebrities, but they can also simply be people who clearly need to be looked after more than most. Sometimes I designate someone a VIP simply because as soon as I see them I know they are high maintenance or could create a problem down the line. You develop an instinct in this business.

Most importantly, VIPs are not always well known to the general public. They might be guests who visit regularly, whose business you want to treasure and keep. Or it might be that friends of the owner, the general manager or head chef are coming for lunch or dinner, and so of course they want them to have the VIP treatment. Albert Roux once told me, 'Fred, if you can't make your boss happy then you can't make anyone happy.' He was so right, and what better way than to look after their friends so well that they report back to your boss, 'Fred, he was amazing! He looked after us so beautifully!' Of course, critics and 'influencers' in the media receive special treatment too, or rather, they receive treatment that makes them feel particularly important.

If one of these people falls victim to the domino effect, then the opposite happens, and it is even worse than usual. So we keep a special eye on the VIPs to ensure that the service they receive is exceptional. In most good restaurants, when one of these people makes a booking – or a booking is made for them – the letters VIP are added beside their name on the reservations list. Therefore staff are made aware that there is not only an important person in the room, but a Very Important Person. This practice has a drawback. If another guest glances at the reservations list at reception, they might be impressed to learn that they will be a table or two from a VIP, but they could also feel miffed that they are not regarded as a VIP.

So you will not see those letters beside anyone's name on my own reservations list. Instead – and I am letting you into a little secret – I prefer to use the letters 'TI'. They stand for Très Important. In these instances I am not asking my staff to go overboard with flamboyant or fawning service. Far from it – sometimes a guest wants the opposite. But sometimes they do want constant attention, to the extent I almost have to take a seat and stay with them for the duration of their meal. 'TI' simply means that the guest should receive that extra little special something: it might be a glass of champagne on the house, or perhaps a dessert at no charge; it might be remembering that they don't like parsley, and flagging up any dishes that contain parsley. It could be a whole world of things, but most of all it is about making sure my team do whatever is necessary to make that particular individual feel as special as possible.

Do not for a moment think that TIs are difficult, pompous or ungrateful. The stars of Hollywood may come from a world of ego pampering and 'yes men', but often they can surprise you with their good manners. When Robert Redford came for dinner at Galvin at Windows he was charming and courteous.

I was not surprised to see that the ladies in the room stopped talking for a moment, their gazes shifting from their husbands towards Mr Redford. Customers went up to him as he enjoyed his meal, and while others might have been irritated by the intrusion, Mr Redford was not. To him, it was not an intrusion. In Mr Redford's case, my job was to protect his right to an undisturbed meal, and ensure he was able to have a good night, despite the obvious interest from the other guests. When a few more people asked if they could have a picture I politely let them know that it was no longer possible. From that point on, Mr Redford was able to focus on his meal.

Recently, one of our guests was an actor who had played James Bond. Of course, he instantly qualified as a TI – who would disagree? He came for a pleasant dinner with his partner and I sat them at a quiet table at the far end of the room, looking out of the floor-to-ceiling window over London, away from prying eyes.

I made sure the table was laid so they could sit with their backs to the room. Mr Bond wanted to enjoy his meal with us, like any other guest, but what he wanted above all was discretion and privacy. To ensure this we also devised a strategic table plan so that the table next to him was gone by the time he arrived. Towards the end of their meal I asked him whether they would like to see the view over London from our outside balcony. To ensure his privacy further I explained I would take him to the balcony via the kitchen as other guests may see him if he took the route through the restaurant.

'I'd love to,' said Bond. As we walked into the kitchen there was a sense of smugness among all of us, front and back of house – James Bond was here, in our kitchen. All of a sudden, a black object fell from his hand and – with lightning reflexes – he bent down and picked it up off the floor. Discussing it later we all felt as if, in that split moment, we were in a scene from a Bond film and 007 had dropped his Walther PPK. Perhaps our imaginations were running pretty wild, but wouldn't yours? He had only dropped his mobile phone, but the chefs expected the bad guys to rush in the kitchen at any moment. I am pleased to say that they did not, instead, we headed out to the balcony, to delight in the view.

Another person on my list of TIs includes Mervyn King, the former governor of the Bank of England. The customer is king, of course, but when he visits this customer is – quite literally – King. He is a charming guest. In 2008, during the middle of the financial crisis, the masterful economist came for dinner. I imagined that he must be deeply burdened by everything that was going on – he was trying to rescue the country from financial collapse, after all. Once dessert had been served, I approached his table. 'I wonder if you would like some herbal tea. We have one with a name that translates as "tea with no worries". I thought it might be helpful at this time.'

He waved a hand in the air, as if to gently shush away the offer. 'Oh thank you, but I don't have any worries.' Once he had guided the nation through the crisis, I saw him again, and asked, 'How did you keep it together?' His response has stayed with me ever since: 'Well, I had a great team of people. It's all about surrounding yourself with great people.' That is true in this business, as well. Although I am the general manager I do not consider myself to be more important than the kitchen porter. He has his role and I have mine, yes, but our shared principles should be the same: looking after the guests and their experience, and protecting the restaurant's reputation and the staff's income, according to the individual responsibilities of your role.

The domino effect illustrates why this is so important. No matter how well set up and ready you are, there will always be hiccups – the food took too long to be served, or perhaps it was never served, or a dish was missed; or a request for a certain table had not been noted during the booking, which has resulted in the customer not being seated in her or his favourite spot; or, when the customer complained, she or he received the 'wrong' response from a waiter or waitress. In every single one of these unfortunate, sometimes inevitable situations, there is only one correct response. We must admit our faults. 'Well, they've got a point. We are the ones at fault. We have let ourselves down.' It is always about acknowledging and then correcting what is wrong. The customer, remember, is king. A sincere apology is essential, of course, but in order to be sincere you must absolutely believe that the fault is yours, and only then will you be able discover what it is that will restore their faith. And as you have seen here, this is different for every customer, particularly the TIs.

I have to use all means – preferably peaceful – to make sure that my staff understand and follow this rule. No matter how much I encourage this culture to be shared, invariably there will be one black sheep who doesn't understand that TI doesn't just mean 'Très Important', but it really means, 'Make no bloody mistakes' – but in stronger language.

17

——●≣

FREE AS A BLUEBIRD

When I left Le Gavroche, London was on the brink of a major restaurant revolution, spearheaded by a man with a game-changing vision: step forwards Sir Terence Conran. An accomplished restaurateur he had opened his first establishment, the Soup Kitchen, in 1953. Shortly afterwards he opened Orrery on the King's Road, and then he would go on to open around 50 restaurants over the next five decades. In the 1990s, Conran really took the London restaurant scene by the scruff of the neck and gave it a good old shake. He launched one restaurant after another, all of them non-elitist and vast – I mean really huge – serving modern food, usually with a Mediterranean influence. The emphasis was always on fresh, well-sourced produce. Extra virgin olive oil, which was moderately new to the British palate, was an essential ingredient of Conran's dishes. London already had a couple of large restaurants: Langan's, just off Piccadilly; and, since late 1992, The Canteen. Set beside the Thames in Chelsea Harbour, it was opened by Marco Pierre White, the actor Michael Caine and Italian restaurateur Claudio Pulze. The Times restaurant critic Jonathan Meades had said to White, 'It sounds like it's going to be a great big canteen. Why don't you call it The Canteen?' And so they did.

Gastrodomes like The Canteen and Conran's Design Museum Café were expensive to build or refurbish, but they could serve thousands of covers every week, which meant – ker-ching! – there were piles of money to be made, if you got it right. There can be no better example of this than Le Pont de La Tour, a large restaurant that was packed from the day it opened. It sits majestically beside the Thames and almost in the shadow of Tower Bridge, and is still busy to this day.

So much of what is taken for granted in today's restaurants can be traced back to Conran and his 1990s gastrodomes, from the freshness and excitement of the food served, to the design and size of the dining rooms. Now there are chains of restaurants with large dining rooms, but these might not have existed were it not for this one man. He changed the way we eat, and gave us restaurants that managed to be both exclusive – celebrities and stars flocked to them – and inclusive (lunches and dinner were not prohibitively expensive).

On Chelsea's world-famous King's Road is a beautiful Art Deco garage. It began life in the 1920s as a garage for the Bluebird Motor Company. There were petrol pumps on the forecourt, and a waiting room for female drivers to use while they waited. Cars were still expensive, and new and innovative measures were being added to the streets of London to prevent poor pedestrians from being run over by motor cars – these were called 'traffic lights'.

The building became an ambulance station and by the mid-1990s it was home to a market that sold trendy clothes and CDs. In 1997 Sir Terence Conran acquired the building and it was a marriage was made in heaven. Conran has a particular talent for design and architecture, a lifelong interest in exceptional food and a long-standing affection for, and association with, this part of London (in the mid-1960s he opened the interiors store Habitat, just along the road).

Conran was the genius at the top, but whenever I think of Bluebird, it is a woman called Wendy Hendricks who comes to mind. Wendy, the general manager, was an Australian who was a few years older than me. She had previously been assistant manager at Quaglino's, another of Conran's hotspots, and now she was in charge of Bluebird, which she oversaw with skills that I had never previously encountered.

Before the launch of the restaurant, I met her for a job interview. She was direct – a straight-talker – who was passionate about service, but also driven by the need for success. I do not recall the specifics, but she knew what she wanted to achieve, and how it should be done. She must also have been talented at interviewing candidates because she brought together the most amazing team of about 100 people.

Each person had a couple of similar traits: first, we were all young; and second, Wendy had taken on interesting characters – we all had a bit of 'life experience'. Many of us had travelled and we were all slightly damaged individuals. For instance, I was recovering from a broken relationship. Wendy quizzed me. 'You were working at Le Gavroche,' said Wendy, my CV on her lap. 'Why did you leave?'

'I felt that I needed a change in my life. I was at Gavroche for a long time. I wanted to do something different, further my career.'

'Why?' she persisted.

'Well, if you really want to know ...'

'I do. That's why I'm asking.'

'My relationship ended ... I felt I wanted to do something else.'

To another employer this might have been a negative. They might have put a line through my name: 'He's preoccupied and damaged. His mind is on other things.' Wendy, however, regarded this as a positive. She could see from my CV that I was as stable as it comes, thanks to the strict way I observed the 12-month rule, and yet the instability of my personal life probably made me more interesting. To Wendy, I had personality.

We were all mavericks. Many of us, as I mentioned, had travelled. For the first time, I was working not with French colleagues, who might be a decade or two older than me, but alongside people who were my own age and they hailed from places as far away as Australia, New Zealand and South Africa. At Le Gavroche, we always talked about France and 'French-ness', and we spoke in French. Many of the staff were in London partly because they wanted to learn English. At Bluebird, we talked in English about surfing and girls and exotic cities and different types of cuisine.

As we all spoke English, we avoided awkward misunderstandings. An old friend of mine from catering college, Joëlle, had recently come to England and was still mastering the language. She was working at Gravetye Manor, a splendid 16th-century mansion and country house hotel, set in the dreamy wilderness of West Sussex. There were two American ladies staying in the hotel and one morning she took breakfast to them in the room they shared. Joëlle carried in the silver tray, and was about to set up a little table for breakfast. One of the ladies glanced at the tray and then she looked at Joëlle and said, 'What about the weather?'

Joëlle was confused. She looked down at the tray: toast, preserves, glasses of orange juice and various other things – she knew the English words for all of them. But what on earth was the weather? She put down the tray and apologised – 'Sorry, sorry … One moment, please …' – and raced downstairs to the kitchen. 'The weather?' said Joëlle to one of the chefs. 'The weather. Where is the weather for the ladies in room 12?' Of course, the ladies were just asking about the forecast, but Joëlle thought part of their order was missing.

There was also a waiter at Le Gavroche. He was extremely tall and skinny, and wore a white tuxedo; he always looked terribly out of place. He had yet to learn English. 'May I have the bill, please?' asked a gentleman. 'Certainly, Sir.' And he scurried away to the kitchen, returning a moment later with a jug of … milk. This sort of confusion could never arise at Bluebird, as all the staff spoke English.

The Bluebird mavericks included Graham who, until a few months earlier, had been an alcoholic living on the streets of London, and spending his nights in a drunken haze on the steps of shops and banks.

I said, 'Graham, why were you homeless?'

'Because I chose to be,' he said. 'It seemed like the right thing to do at the time. Then I got myself back on track.'

There was not a single dull soul among us. No one was normal. Wendy's assistant Craig told me, 'We have personalities coming into this restaurant. We want personalities to serve them.'

This was a startling revelation to me: that the waiter could be anything other than subservient; that the waiter could have a proper conversation with the customer. Wendy had chosen a team of people, each of whom was mostly stable and competent, but with a little touch of madness. We were an anti-establishment, left-wing bunch, who liked Oasis and Blur, the Britpop superstars of the moment.

This colourful collection of characters ensured that there was already a buzz in the room even before the customers arrived; there was a happy atmosphere and a sense of fun as we served dishes such as pan-fried sea bream with spinach, and a generous slice of lemon. There was vibrancy in every part of Bluebird, from the customers and staff, to the design and décor and, of course, the food.

The setting was ideal. The restaurant looked onto the street, and was airy and spacious with high, expansive windows, and even more natural light streaming in from the skylight – quite a contrast to the opulent gloom of Le Gavroche. I had moved, physically and figuratively, from the dark into the light.

There were enough tables to seat several hundred people. At one end of the room, close to reception, there was a cocktail bar. At the other end, there was a crustacean bar, which was manned by a couple of chefs. It was huge, appetising and colourful, with lobsters, crabs, langoustines, mussels and clams all laid out on crushed ice.

The Bluebird opened just at the right time. The UK was coming out of recession and people were in the mood for change, for light, fun, unstuffy experiences. Tony Blair had just become prime minister. He was young and extremely popular; the future looked promising and the nation was in high spirits. Bluebird was like a club by the sea, the tempting scent of hedonism hanging in the air. It was no surprise then that most of us were desperate to get into work in the morning.

On that first morning, all of us waiters stood shoulder to shoulder in that big, bright room, watching as Wendy's assistant Craig – a fit, tall, young Australian with closely-cropped hair – paced up and down. He spoke slowly, clearly and loudly. Boy, was he confident! 'I bloody love this job,' he said. (His accent turned bloody into blardy.) 'I dream about it. I live it. I blardy breathe it!' He spoke with passion, and the passion was infectious. In another life, he could have been an army captain preparing his troops before the charge, over the top, and into battle. Or a slick Wall Street dealer on the trading floor, geeing up his pinstriped team seconds before the clang of the morning bell.

As assistant manager, Craig was delivering the daily briefing. With each word he pumped up his captivated audience: 40 or 50 young waiters and waitresses, energised and inspired by his words, and ready for service as if nothing else mattered. Because nothing else did matter. As head waiter, I hung on to his every word.

To the outside world, Craig's briefings might have seemed

trivial. To us, they were life-affirming, rallying speeches that raised our spirits and propelled us forwards. Until then I had only known the French restaurant style of briefing: clear, concise, just focusing on the specials of the day and the cheeses, what wine goes with what, and that sort of thing. Craig's speeches were on another level altogether. The Chinese say that the bluebird is the harbinger of happiness, and that is precisely what this restaurant would bring to my life.

'I blardy breathe this job,' Craig repeated, as he walked up and down in front of us. 'And you know what I absolutely love?' People shook their heads. What did Craig absolutely love? 'You know what I love more than anything?' No, what did he love more than anything? He darted to the tables of two, beside one of the windows that overlooked the King's Road. 'I love tables of two,' he said. 'Because with tables of two, you can go bang, bang, bang!'

As he spoke, he moved his hands as if he was quickly setting the tables, and then resetting them with the same speed. 'This is how you do tables of two. You feed the customers, and then you reset. Fast. Easy. No fuss. No mess.' We nodded. 'Quick and fast.' There was a pause, as we all nodded excitedly, 'Larger tables take time. But tables of two are so easy.'

As we settled into the fast rhythm at Bluebird, I remained in awe of Wendy and the way she controlled the room. She had the most alluring presence on the floor, forever smiling. She was never reluctant to be honest: to praise you if you were right; correct you if you were wrong. She had the total confidence of the people above her, including Sir Terence. We knew that she was trusted and, in our eyes, this added to her gravitas. Wendy was always impeccably dressed with her hair cut into an immaculate brunette bob. Wendy was always there and never once did she have a bad day.

But she did have a naughty side. Like me, Wendy could be a bit cheeky. Sometimes she could go beyond what might be perceived as correct form. One day, I remember her talking to me and, in a tactile way, holding my forearm. No doubt she wanted to make a point, and the physical touch was a way of reinforcing it. Wanting to have a bit of fun, I said, 'Wendy, it's a long time since a girl held me like this. And I'm quite enjoying it.' She looked at me in horror. I was overstepping the mark, but then, she had started it. Her grip loosened and she went cold. I had seen a rare glimpse beyond Wendy the professional, but only for a second,

As well as a new kind of energy, there were also modern forms of technology to master. Or, at least, for me to master. I was used to paper and pen. Now I was using computers, and the point-of-service till system. The touch of a few buttons, and the kitchen received the order. Great stuff! It took me about a month to learn how to use it well and I have never looked back.

We had 'runners' who brought the dishes from the kitchen, and whisked the empty plates away. My assistant, Sandra, had two memorable attributes. She was beautiful – dark haired, dark features, gorgeous smile – and she hated her job. This was a shame as she was excellent at it. Blessed with a remarkable memory she only ever needed to be told something once. She was also a highly capable actress, so unless she told you that she hated her job, you would have thought that she had found her life's vocation in waitressing.

The whole team was a regiment of determined young people, out to do a fantastic job of serving the customers, whether they liked it or not. The customers were often similar in age to the waiting staff, and they came for a particularly good time, beginning with expensive Champagne at the bar, followed by a ludicrously long lunch, and cocktails at the bar afterwards. They could keep it up all day and all night long, with money no object.

My social life picked up, too. The gloom of splitting from my partner evaporated as I made new friends at Bluebird. There were about a dozen of us who used to hang out, finishing the shift on Sundays, and then heading off to Clerkenwell to a club called Turnmills that was well known for its crazy raves. On Sundays there was a gay night, which was the best night of the week. Only one of us was gay, but we all piled along because it was extreme entertainment and, remember, we were hedonists. There were also lots of girls there – there's never a better place to meet girls than in a gay club. It was a hardcore night with loads of drugs and near-naked men writhing about on the sweaty dance floor. I was really into the fast, loud techno house music. Of course, we were all exhausted. Sometimes I would actually fall asleep at a table, wake up 20 minutes later, and get back onto the dance floor. There was a banner on the wall that declared, 'Time is irrelevant.'

For our motley crew – the dirty dozen from Bluebird – London was a place of bohemian tests and trials. We were far from home, beyond the scrutiny and finger-pointing of family and friends, and we could do what we liked. We were beginning to talk about our aspirations and our goals in life, yet we were living in the moment, never considering that middle age would catch up with us. We were without our families, but – clichéd though it may sound – we became one big family.

At Bluebird there was an all-pervading feeling of friendliness, and this atmosphere was all thanks to Wendy. I also learned something fundamental from her: in order to create a successful large restaurant you must run it as a small restaurant.

When you think about it, a small restaurant is intimate or 'personal', and endearingly so. A large restaurant is often impersonal, usually because there are no personalities. Personalities create the personal touch. That was why Wendy had wanted so many of us, all with our own particular characters, to be greeting the customers, waiting at the tables and serving the food and wine. In a small restaurant, you will frequently find that almost every member of staff cares about quality. Think, for instance, of those wonderful family-run restaurants, where you are met and well fed – and entertained – by the husband, wife and their children. The Bluebird was vast – still is – but at the same time it was so intimate. And all this intimacy was coupled with delivering excellent food at a terrific pace. Of course, at Le Gavroche, dishes had to be delivered swiftly, but we all knew you could not rush a soufflé. At Bluebird, everything was quick – but everything was still absolutely delicious.

Terence Conran would pop in, enveloped in his own aura of magnificence. I was not even born when he became a big shot. He was always very kind and respectful towards the staff, having a glass of Chablis, sharing ideas and saying what he wanted to say. In particular, he knew exactly what he wanted on the plate. His restaurants were there to feed and entertain, but they were also there to make money.

———◀═

The front-of-house team did not really mix socially with the chefs. We were such a big pack anyway, and there was never any time. There is, however, one chef who sticks in my mind. He was about 15 years older than me, and had been drafted in by Conran to help with the launch of Bluebird. His name was Chris Galvin.

Just like the rest of us, he had real personality along with a slightly damaged background. He was born and raised in Essex but his love of food came from an unforgettable childhood holiday in France. His dad had won big on the horses one day, and used the cash to buy a second-hand Vauxhall Viva. This was in the days before Benidorm and the European package holiday. The family stopped at places recommended in the restaurant guide Les Routiers, and even though Chris's parents didn't speak a word of French, they all fell in love with France. The family's visits across the Channel became an annual event: motoring through the countryside; sleeping in the car; and eating food bought at markets or *les plats du jour* in cafés and bistros. They ate simple dishes of Steak Frites or Blanquette de Veau, but these were enough to ignite Chris's passion for food.

Meanwhile, his life in Romford, Essex, was filled with more food adventures. His grandmother had a garden that had helped feed her and her nine children during the Second World War. She grew different varieties of potato, as well as cauliflowers and rhubarb; there were also pear and apple trees and gooseberry bushes; and chickens produced plenty of eggs. It was great to hear Chris talk about that small paradise, where his grandmother taught him about seasonality: 'No, don't eat that, it will give you a sore belly; it's not ready. That's ready, this is ready.' His favourite hobby was scrumping – pinching fruit from the trees – an activity at which he excelled and was the leader of a gang of young scrumpers. 'I knew where the great apples or pears were,' he told me.

He enjoyed cookery at school – unlike today, at that time it was unusual for boys to show an interest in cooking, although they may have secretly yearned to be in the kitchen. Those heady days of youth came to a abrupt end when Chris was 15 years old and his father walked out on the family – 'He disappeared.' The Galvins were left to struggle with little money. Chris's mother was seriously ill and, it looked as if the children – Chris, his younger brothers Dave, nine, and Jeff, three – would be taken into care. Other members of the family stepped in to help out, and were able to stop the mother and her children from being separated.

Chris became the man of the house. 'I knocked on the door of a restaurant,' he says. 'I got a job washing up and that was everything for me. It was warm, it was an instant family. There was food. The sous chef was Antony Worrall Thompson and, you know, he looked after me. I got three quid a session, a fiver on Saturdays. And I got my brother a job and my Mum a job. I just loved it. It was all I wanted to do,' he said. Antony was brilliant and on his way up in the world, and he began to let Chris put food on the plates. Antony started telling the head chef, 'You don't have to come in on Saturday. It's alright John, me and Chris are going to do service.'

What Chris especially liked was 'looking after people'. 'I think as a chef', he has told me, 'one of the most important things to me is … giving something to someone and sharing.' Soon he dreamt of owning a restaurant and strived to learn everything he possibly could. Antony Worrall Thompson guided him to London, where he worked for Michael Quinn in the kitchens of The Ritz. The hotel, in turn, paid for him to go to catering school, where he excelled and became student of the year. He felt as if he had arrived and, after a stint at L'Escargot in Soho, he was working for Conran.

———⊨

The thrill of Bluebird continued, day after day, for six months. But then, on a chilly morning in the autumn of 1997, it came to a sudden end. Wendy Hendricks gathered us together and, rather than delivering an upbeat, bonding, go-get-'em briefing, she announced, 'I just wanted to let you all know that I am leaving.' We were stunned. How could she leave? How could she leave us? 'It has been brilliant working with you all', she said. 'And I do hope our paths cross again.'

I stayed for a year after Wendy's departure, but I am not quite sure why. Perhaps I hoped that life would continue just as it had always been, but I was wrong. Wendy was replaced, but the problem was she was unbeatable, unmatchable, irreplaceable. After she left, the hierarchy became elitist, the front-of-house discipline fell apart and the quest for excellence vanished. The respect I had for my boss disappeared.

Perhaps the new managers did not love Bluebird enough. It is all very well to say, 'I want the quality to be high.' But to achieve excellent quality, you must be genuinely obsessed with it. Then that determination will spread through the ranks, and everyone will work together. But when the obsession is lacking at the top, staff merely pitch up to do their shifts and life becomes methodical, as it did when Wendy left. The culture, which had been so lovingly established and then nurtured by Wendy, suffered a slow and painful death. Yes, it was gone, but as far as I am concerned, it has never been forgotten.

18

THE CRITICS

My time at Bluebird also brought me into contact with that feared part of the food world: the restaurant critic. In those days, critics were not too concerned about reviewing Michelin-starred restaurants – their job had already been done by Michelin. If a critic had come to Le Gavroche during my time there, then it was probably to have a good meal rather than write a review. They were treated exactly like anyone else: immaculately, of course, but not as TIs.

If we got wind that a critic was coming to Bluebird it was a whole different story. Red alert! Red alert! Wendy and assistant Craig would amass the troops for a briefing, with the adrenaline pump at hand, as usual, and off they'd go.

'Okay guys, listen up. This is a biggie. Fay Maschler is definitely coming for dinner one day this week. We've gotta look after her. We've gotta make her feel special. We've gotta make sure she has an experience like she's never had. That food has gotta be beautiful. You have to be brilliant and you have to be kind. Make her feel like she's the greatest person in the world. And maybe she is. No one messes with Fay Maschler.'

We all cheered. When the cheering died down, I said, 'Craig, sorry ... Fay Mash-who?' I had much to learn. I don't remember Fay's review in the *Evening Standard*, but I imagine it was glowing as at Bluebird business only seemed to thrive.

In the old days, critics were revered and, up to a point, that is still the case, even as their influence has waned with the ascent of social media. Nowadays anyone with a camera phone and a blog can be a critic. You may not know their name, but they might have thousands, or even hundreds of thousands, of loyal followers, relying on them for their next great meal. Or, they might have three followers. Some bloggers and Instagrammers are true gourmands – they have passion, knowledge and they really care. You can always tell who they are because for them it isn't about getting a free meal: they are there for the food, for the service, to explore and marvel at the wonder that is eating out. Others are ... not very good, let's put it that way, and don't know what they are talking about. We restaurant managers are bombarded by their emails:

'Hi, I'm a professional blogger, and here is a link to my blog. I have three followers, my mum, my dad and my little brother, who is 15 years old. I would like to come and review your restaurant. There will be four of us. If you want me to write a good review let me know and I'll come in on a complimentary basis.'

Like hell, you will! But of course, I could never reply in that way. So, I have developed a strategy. Either I do not reply, or

I send a response along the lines of: 'Thank you very much, but we can't do it.' Another restaurant might be more generous and accommodating, but I think that if you want to eat here, whether you are reviewing or not, you will understand that we run a business and we need to make money. There is no such thing as a free lunch!

There is no doubt that the voice of the 'authentic' critic has been diluted by the bloggers but I feel that this dilution is slower than we might imagine. The critics who write for national newspapers and magazines still wield a great deal of power, which bloggers have not yet managed to replicate. Think of the late, great AA Gill, restaurant critic for *The Sunday Times*. His words would direct readers to the doors of certain restaurants, and away from others. Why? Because he was more than just a critic. His column appeared on a Sunday, and in this country the Sunday papers are a real ritual. So, he became an essential part of many people's Sunday routine. Of course, there was also the fact that his prose was unique; beautifully delivered with the mightiest pen, as entertaining as it was exciting. I remember when Jeremy Clarkson came to Galvin at Windows and we had a fun chat on the balcony. He was having a good laugh dissing – in the most affectionate terms – AA Gill. 'Adrian hates everything he eats,' said Jeremy, 'so I haven't got a clue where to take him anymore.'

Gill leaves a massive void – no blogger or other critic has as distinctive a voice. Nevertheless, every mainstream paper has a restaurant critic whose writing is compelling even to a reader who has little interest in restaurants or does not eat out. They have to write that well to keep their place in the fast-changing world of the newsroom. And so, the critics are still feared. As the waiter or restaurateur you want to please them. You want them to like what you do, of course, because if they write positively then you end up with a glowing, lengthy article that is a vindication and confirmation of the fine work that you do. And of course, a great review means that people will absolutely come to your restaurant.

However, I always think it is very important to remember that when a critic is eating in a restaurant they are reviewing, they are at work. He is looking at the plate from a technical point of view, constantly analysing, as opposed to chilling out and enjoying the experience. Sometimes this can be detrimental – blowing things out of proportion and making mountains out of molehills – but still, the professional and skilled critic should be able to disassociate the work from the pleasure, combining the critical part of the process with the enjoyment.

A good critic sets out to be neither deliberately negative nor positive. That is why I will never give a meal in exchange for a good review. That would not be genuine. Instead, I feel that a critic must be objective and simply tell it like it is, whether that is good or bad.

As a reader, you might wince when you see a terrible review. 'I will not go to that restaurant,' you might say to yourself. Or you might think, 'It sounds dreadful, but I'm curious, so I'll try it.' And if you are a nice person, you might feel sorry for the restaurant, too. However, there is so much jealousy in this business you can bet your life that at the same time that ghastly critique is being read by rival restaurateurs, and that they are thoroughly delighted to see a competitor being panned. The Germans have a name for it – *schadenfreude*: the pleasure derived from someone else's misfortune.

———€

I was quite amused when I read Jay Rayner's now-infamous critique of Le Cinq, the restaurant within the Hotel Georges V in Paris. Now, Le Cinq is not just any old restaurant. It has three Michelin stars, which it has held for many years, and as such is unused to anything but glowing reviews.

Rayner's review, which appeared in the Observer in the spring of 2017, gave the restaurant a real pummelling. He called his meal in this so-called shrine to gastronomy '... by far the worst restaurant experience I have endured in my 18 years in this job'. I was particularly stunned by the effect this review had on other critics. The French writers rounded on Rayner; critics who always call for more freedom, more space to be blunt and honest and speak the truth, were almost united in outrage at someone else doing the same. Rayner became the subject of criticism by the critics, all because he had done exactly what a critic is supposed to do: eaten a meal somewhere, made a judgement and passed this judgement on to his readers. There was a lot of discussion about the fact that he was English, and therefore did not understand what proper food should be. But in criticising him in this way, these critics went against their very raison d'être, and I found this extremely ironic.

When all is said and done, Jay Rayner is just a man; he goes out to eat and he has an opinion, like you or I. His opinion is no more valid than my opinion or your opinion (or indeed the opinion of the French critics who disagreed with him). Yes, he has a column in the *Observer* and an extremely healthy following on Twitter. Whatever he writes is widely read, retweeted and commented upon, and therefore further increases his fame or the interest in what he has to say. But let's face it, he is merely one man, whose opinion was that he had a very bad meal indeed. I wasn't there, and neither were you, and we cannot comment on Le Cinq until we have been. You can't be up in arms because an English critic had a bad meal, and that bad meal happened to be in France. I find that laughable.

When I read Rayner's review I immediately thought of my own worst meal. It was also in a three-star Michelin restaurant somewhere in the South of France, although I am not going to tell you which city. I was on a PR trip and we were there to sample various ingredients, meet fishermen, local growers and wine producers. We were travelling around with a view to finding new ideas we could bring back with us to London.

We went to the restaurant quite early in the day, not to eat but to meet the chef-patron and have a chat, again for inspiration. Time was against us, and we called the restaurant to say that we were running late and apologised. When we finally arrived, the chef was in the garden of the restaurant. Despite our profuse apologies, he had the hump and was upset that we were so late.

He should have said 'Look, I'm sorry guys, you're here and I'm pleased, but I'm afraid the timing is off. I've got to prep now.' Or he could have sent somebody to tell us the same thing. Instead, he saw us and then spent the whole time moaning about it in French to me, which made translating for my companions rather awkward.

We all left thinking, 'What an idiot! This is supposed to be the hospitality business and he is the man leading from the front, the chef-patron.' We had arrived expecting to be inspired, but we left feeling desperately disappointed. Worse, we would have to return later on, because we were booked in for dinner that evening.

In the meantime, we had lunch with a family of wine producers. It was one of those unexpected feasts that you never forget. The hospitality was second to none, the Mediterranean sun shone, and we finished off the meal sitting in the shade of a tree, smoking cigars, sniffing cognac, and savouring the blissful moments – with not a Michelin star in sight.

After freshening up at our hotel, we returned to the three-star restaurant to eat. We were a bit reluctant, I must admit. What followed was the menu dégustation of 15, or was it 20, courses. The food was okay but we still had that bitter taste in our mouths from the morning garden encounter with the chef.

I must confess that we had arrived late – again – for dinner, which upset the staff. I understand – you have a table plan to execute, guests arriving late is annoying. But you cannot ever let the customer see this! I found it difficult to focus on the conversation at our table because I could hear the waiters talking behind me in French, moaning about our lateness. At one point a waiter was serving the water as he stood behind us and he poured the water into an empty wine glass, rather than the water glass. Okay, it can happen. He got the wrong glass – it's no big deal – but he inhaled dramatically when he realised, so that everyone on our table had to stop talking and feel anxious on his behalf. That is not the way to put your customers at ease.

As the meal continued, the waiters' voices behind me droned on and on. They moaned that the dishes would be delayed, and that clearly we weren't real restaurant professionals, otherwise we would never have been late. This restaurant was unbelievable, but for all the wrong reasons. In fact, we ended up leaving quite late because the food was so slow to be served, and service really dragged. It was not a pleasant experience. Or to use Rayner's word, it was awful. And all with three Michelin stars!

Now, if you read the reviews about that restaurant, I am sure you will find plenty of good ones. In fact, I had been to the restaurant a couple of years earlier and had eaten well on that occasion. But I will never go back because my more recent experience was so unsatisfactory.

I don't remember a single one of the dishes we ate, even though there were 15 (or 20), because they were – in my view – very ordinary. Service can make such a different to the taste of things. The food alone is not enough. There has to be the right ambiance, the whole package. The service was lacking and so the food tasted mediocre. It is the domino effect again: everything is connected, and good food is nothing without a good waiter.

———

The critic arrived at reception with his guests. I recognised him because I had come across him – briefly – once before. The table that I had intended for him was still occupied; the people had not left yet. Now, I knew he was particular, partly through reputation and also because of his sheer presence as I laid eyes on him, so I needed to think on my feet. This man absolutely did not want anything to be ordinary or run of the mill.

I have talked about never leaving a customer alone with his thoughts. That is definitely true in the case of this type of guest; you definitely want him to know you are there for him.

We had only one table free at the time and so I sat him there. I said, 'I have another table planned for you, but the guests are still finishing their dessert. But they will be going soon. They've asked for coffee and they've asked for the bill. But I want you to have a good time so rather than make you wait I've ordered a few dishes. They are to share amongst yourselves and as soon as the other table is ready, I will move you there, take your order and you can have a good time.'

'Oh, thank you,' he said. 'Thank you.' Two or three dishes went to his table. There is much to be said about giving something for free, but the message was more to do with me thinking about him, what he wanted and about his motivation. How did he want to be treated over and above everybody else? You could say that the food critic has a sense of entitlement, but I think you need to focus on the individual.

There are guests who indeed have that sense of entitlement, and others who require no fuss and do not mind, for instance, if they have to wait for a table. This was a person who wanted to be treated slightly better than everybody else. He also happened to be a food critic, that's all. So his table not being ready for him was a rare experience for him, not dissimilar to Jay Rayner's visit to Le Cinq where everything was hopeless, and mine to the three-star establishment in the South of France. In this case, however, I was determined to make sure that he had the best time possible, despite the inauspicious start.

I moved him and his guests to the other table, and we proceeded with normal service. Once he was seated at the new table he did not want to talk to me. We have a saying in French, 'Je suis aux petit soins.' It means I am tending to your every need. I had done that. The critic felt that he was the only one in the room, and that I was looking after him with such care that it did not matter about anybody else. He was comforted and immersed in the sort of hospitality that he felt he deserved; it was what felt right for him. Once this had been established, my presence was no longer required.

Just before he left, he said, 'Fred, it was amazing. You must be the best maître d' in the country.' Six months later the restaurant won an award for its impeccable service. It was all down to the way my staff and I treated him during that visit. We won because I recognised him, as a food critic, yes, but also as someone who needed to be looked after in a very specific way. The signs were all there and flashing. If you fail to heed these warning signs then, I am sorry to say, you are a maître d' with no eyes, no ears and no feelings.

There are different types of critic and each has his or her own requirements. Inspectors of restaurant guides have a very straightforward requirement: they must arrive incognito and remain unidentified during their meal. Just as some people simply want to be extravagantly looked after, some critics like Marina O'Loughlin want to remain anonymous (or have to), which I think is another great way to truly get a sense of a restaurant. Think about it. If you cannot treat an anonymous person in the best way possible, you imply that you run a place where a guest has to be a somebody to get anything – and that is the antithesis of hospitality, isn't it?

In the old days, however, the inspectors were easy to spot, despite their best efforts. They tended to book a table for one, and would order no more than a half bottle of wine. They liked to eat dinner early, and would not spend too long at the table. That's a very rare and specific sort of customer in the world of fine dining. Nowadays, however, the inspectors can also arrive en masse; there might be not just two of them, but three or four. Sometimes they come on bank holidays, and they always still book under an alias – just to be on the safe side. Occasionally they do make themselves known to the manager or restaurant owner. They tell you who they are and ask questions about the restaurant and the menu. They rarely give feedback about their experience … until you read it in print.

Even when I clock the inspectors, I do not worry, because to me, a visit from them is just another table with guests who need to be looked after and receive the best possible customer service. There is a secret database of restaurant managers and a group email is sent to this select group: 'We had an inspector in today and his name is X.' It keeps everyone on their guard, just in case an inspector calls. It's always useful to know.

In terms of dealing with critics, what matters most is the correct ethos pumping through the veins of every single member of staff. That way they can spot who needs what and how to deliver it, and make everybody feel good and comfortable, whether they are a high-maintenance critic, or an anonymous one, or just someone who is there for a wonderful meal. On that basis, you will be always come out on top, no matter who your guests are. For if you really think about it, every guest is a critic. They may only tell a couple of friends, but then those friends could talk to their friends, who could talk to their friends, and so on, and so on …

19

PUBLIC RELATIONS

Only the foolish restaurateur fails to recognise the importance of public relations or PR. This is a relatively new phenomenon – not many people bothered with it in the 1980s or early 1990s. Now, you cannot move for specialist foodie PR companies in London. In my opinion, their aim should be to spread the news from your business far and wide, making sure absolutely everyone has heard about it. At its heart, PR is searching for ways to get your story across and ensure that you are 'relevant', and that people are interested with what you have to say.

There are so many ways to do this but from my experience, which is shared by colleagues and friends of mine, for the most part PR companies tend to be uncreative and rarely have a brilliant idea. The motto of the SAS is 'Who Dares Wins'; far too often PRs do not dare and so cannot win. Instead of relying on real creativity, light-bulb moments and innovative events and ideas, they conjure up notions that are so ridiculously complicated that they end up being entirely disconnected with how the restaurant is run. A team will beaver away on an idea that will result in only a couple of column inches in London's free newspapers, such as *Metro* or the *Evening Standard*. Only a small number of people are likely to read such a small article, and the take-up – the number of people who will book a table as a result – will be negligible. So what are we paying thousands of pounds for? To my mind restaurant PR needs to shift its thinking and become more agile, focusing entirely on events that will demonstrate a concrete return – after all, this is what we pay for!

I remember working with a particular PR company and whenever I made a suggestion – Who Dares Wins, remember – they would say to me, 'Well, you know, it's a good idea but you're not quite Gordon Ramsay, are you? So, there's only so much we can do.' For them, it was about managing expectations. It got to a point where I said, 'Well, it is true, I am not Gordon Ramsay. But I have been punching above my weight all my life and I continue to do so. And I win! You've got to believe, you've got to make it happen. If you try and you fail then at least you have tried. But if you put me down straight away before I've even started, what chance do I have?' I'm sure you will not be surprised to hear that it was not long before they lost a client.

Proper moments of PR feel fun and exciting; they are always about so much more than just a tweet or an email. Shortly after we opened Galvin at Windows in 2007, my mother happened to mention that there would be 13 full moons in the year, rather than the usual 12. I became fascinated by this and decided to celebrate it with a nice bit of PR. It is said that years with 13 full moons are accompanied by strange weather, so at the time of booking we asked customers to guess what the weather would be when they came for their meal. If they were correct, they won a bottle of Champagne. Journalists wrote about the stunt; it had a good angle which wasn't just about getting bookings up, it was about having fun and making the experience even better for the customer. As a result, the take-up was pretty impressive. When customers turned up for lunch or dinner, if their predictions were correct then they won a bottle of Champagne. Sometimes it would start raining halfway through a sunny lunch – so whether you said rain or sun, you won. The corks were popping incessantly for a month. As Shakespeare said, 'Though this be madness, yet there is method in't.'

With the rise and rise of social media, there are now companies who will tweet for you, for a fee, naturally. Let me tell you something about social media: you can do it anywhere. In bed, on the toilet, on the train. So why would you pay a PR company to do something so simple? What is more, a PR agency can never know as much about your restaurant as you do, unless they are there all day, every day, watching who is visiting and what the customers are really responding to. Simply tweeting the menu, or a new dish, is never enough. There are two levels of social media: first, broadcasting, which is to say getting your message out there and online; and second, and this is where the power lies, connecting with your followers. So, if someone replies to your post about the menu, say, then the really important thing is to reply to them, in a non-automated manner. How can a PR agency be better placed to be the voice of your restaurant than someone who works there? Restaurateurs are in the best place to tweet about

Galvin at Windows because they are totally absorbed in the restaurant's vision, values and ethos.

So what is the solution? If you have a PR on board, because you are already too busy with the more immediate parts of running a restaurant, you have to crack the whip every day. The PR sits at a desk, sends an email and then thinks, 'I've sent an email. Isn't that amazing? Job done', without looking for any more of a result, or any kind of follow up. Well, that isn't enough, is it? My immediate reaction is to ask, 'What was the reply? Was there a reply? If there is no reply, who do we go to next? Should we chase?' Or a PR might say, 'I can get Giles Coren/ Grace Dent/Marina O'Loughlin to come and write a review of your restaurant, if you pay me and take on my company to do your PR.' Well, I recommend taking this with a barrow-load of salt. These critics have integrity, and would not dream of doing such a thing. They cannot be bought. The fact is, if the restaurant is good then the critics will come, like moths to a flame. That is what critics do: search for good restaurants and go and eat in them. That is the most important part of their job, and no amount of PR is going to suddenly persuade them to go to this place or that.

———

We were one of the first restaurants of Michelin calibre to invest our energies into social media. In fact, as a result of our success, Hilton devised a social media policy for the whole company. One of the main reasons for this is that about nine years ago I went to Twestival, which heralded the beginning of Twitter. I was there to award some prizes – Champagne here, a meal there – and talked to followers from Twitter IRL ('in real life'), as they say. I met this guy who was on Twitter and was a filmmaker, and while we were chatting, I had an idea. 'I want to do a live Champagne and oyster tasting at Galvin at Windows. We'll have all sorts of interesting people who will come along and I want to broadcast it live on the Internet.' His eyes lit up. There were a few people doing similar broadcasts in parts of the United States and Canada, but in London it had not been done and never by a restaurant.

My new friend was definitely up for it so I invited all sorts of bloggers to the event. Remember that bloggers were not very well known at the time, so this might have been perceived as a risk – who would be watching, anyway? Nigel Barden, the food and drink presenter from the BBC, was the host. There was a blind tasting of a range of top-brand Champagnes, including Laurent-Perrier, and there was also a Spanish Cava thrown in as a wild card, and we served oysters from a top seafood restaurant. I am still amazed to say that when the blind tasting was finished, and it was time to announce the winner, the Spanish Cava came out on top. The internet blew up! What did we learn? Well, it was worth taking a risk. There was no obvious return, but I strongly believed that the event would pay off in the long run, and it has. It helped us forge relationships with bloggers who are now hugely influential. I knew them before they are who they are now; we have grown together. The thing is, we dared, and so we won. And Cava won, too.

20

———🍴———

KING GEORGE AND
THE GOO-GOOS

After I left Bluebird, I had a short stint in New York before opening Brasserie Roux on Pall Mall. When it was time to leave the Brasserie, I felt a bit lost, so I turned to the person I most admired during my time at Bluebird for advice. Wendy said some invaluable things which I still remember to this day. 'Think of your CV and what you've already done,' she said. 'At your age, you should stay in the West End, because once you leave you won't be able to come back. You might get a job as a manager elsewhere,' added Wendy, 'but it's better to be an assistant manager and stay in the West End.' 'Qui peut le plus peut le moins', as God had told me years earlier. Then she added, 'I do know someone who's looking for an assistant manager. You should go and see him.'

Wendy was steering me towards one of the most endearing non-conformists of the West End restaurant scene during the

1990s. George Perendes was a total maverick and a hugely loveable rogue. He also ran another jewel in Conran's crown: Sartoria on Savile Row. They served well-made Italian cuisine: white crab meat with parsley, garlic and a splash of olive oil; tagliatelle with grated truffle; a handsome grilled veal chop with spinach and fried courgettes. This was served at Mayfair prices to a clientele of elegant shoppers, wealthy tourists and business people who were guests in the nearby five-star hotels. George was older than me by at least ten years, and had a long history in the trade. He had a delicious, dry sense of humour, with perfect deadpan delivery and a relaxed aura, which sent out the message that nothing could faze him. I liked him from our first meeting, where he offered me the job of assistant manager on the spot.

I arrived at 9am, ready to start the first day of my new life. Everything was going smoothly and then the doors opened for lunch. George, who had previously spoken to me in a London accent, now greeted guests with an Italian accent, but he was Greek! Guests breezed through the door, one after the other, to be met by oodles of Italian charm from George. He switched his nationality as he saw fit; one moment he sounded like a Londoner, the next he could have been a Roman. It was clear from those opening moments of that first lunch service that the guests adored him. He was warm, funny, considerate, and hawk-eyed. As he moved around the room, from table to table, smiling and chatting, his accent crossed countries faster than Concorde: he treated every single guest exactly as they wished to be treated. Sartoria was George's realm, and he was king. Waiters hung on his every word, too. He could crook a finger towards the bar, the kitchen, or the cloakroom, and a waiter would immediately scurry over to do his bidding.

I felt as if I was watching a magician at work, and when I went home in the early hours of the following morning, I was extremely relieved that I had taken Wendy's advice and stayed in the heart of London.

———⊏

George needed to teach me the ropes, of course. Every manager has his own style of leadership and his own philosophy. George, I would discover, was distinctly different to any other boss I had come across. His assessment of lower waiting staff was somewhat unconventional. He called them the 'goo-goos'. When I first heard him say it, I was confused. I said, 'George, the what? The goujons?'

'The goo-goos.'

'What are the goo-goos, George?'

'Not what,' he said. 'But who?'

'Okay. Who are the goo-goos?'

George took a drag on his cigarette, lifted a hand and waved it towards the waiters and waitresses who were working around us: they were hoovering the floors, setting tables and ironing white linen tablecloths. 'You're looking at them. The goo-goos are all around us,' said George.

The goo-goos were his minions: the chefs de rang, and below them the waiters and the busboys. At Sartoria, they were mostly from overseas, and unlike at Bluebird, they did not speak good English. As a Briton, you might say a goo-goo was not the sharpest tool in the box. A Frenchman might say 'Il n'a pas inventé le fil à couper le beurre' – he did not invent the wire that slices the butter.

George hired these people deliberately, because then he could be in complete control. These people were all brilliant at doing exactly what he wanted them to do. He just had to show them, and then they would do it, no discussions or arguments or backchat. What followed over the coming weeks provided a new and unique insight into staff training and development. By hiring goo-goos, George cleverly acquired a regiment of waiting staff who could be moulded and shaped into adequate waiters or waitresses. They never complained, argued or caused a fuss. He told me, 'I make myself strong by getting everybody strong. The more I have to do, the worse you and everyone else is at doing their jobs.' It was a contrast to Silvano's philosophy at Le Gavroche, but interestingly they both worked.

As with every great restaurant, at Sartoria there were daily briefings. Of course, they were completely different to any that I had seen previously. About half an hour before every lunch and dinner service, George stood in the centre of the dining room. He would then explain in precise detail what he wanted everyone to do during service. There were mini demonstrations, with George acting the part of the guest or the waiter as appropriate. Occasionally the goo-goos would take part in the role playing, with George directing. 'Right,' he'd say at the end of the briefing, 'have a good service. Get to your stations.' And the goo-goos would scuttle off in all directions, awaiting the first guests.

There were a couple of loose cannons. These included Giuseppe, a small guy from Naples who could barely speak five words of English. The five words he knew were the ones he used when he addressed the guests at the table: 'Hey! What do you want?' It was incredibly frustrating to observe Giuseppe barking gruffly as he took the orders, 'Hey! What do you want?' From the centre of the room, George would look slightly pained, as he stared at Giuseppe in desperation. At times, he said, 'You know Giuseppe, you are only here because you make me laugh ... Right, go and polish the plates.' Giuseppe would slope away but never to polish the plates, of course, because he couldn't understand a word George was saying.

For a while the kitchen was run by John, an excellent chef with a difficult temperament. Sometimes he would leave the stove downstairs and appear on the restaurant floor, screaming obscenities about anything and everything. George would rush to the scene. 'Calm down,' he would say, before gently leading John back to the kitchen for a soothing chat, or, on bad days, a slanging match.

George also had his own way of doing the staff rota, which determined who worked which shift. Usually, it is the heads of department who do the rota for their own staff, but George did not follow that system. Once a week, on an afternoon in between lunch and dinner service, he would sit down at a table in the empty restaurant, to work out the days on which every single one of his staff would work.

His rota was something to behold – lengthy manuscripts full of names, job titles, dates and times – that covered the entire table. The whole thing took hours. For each service, he needed managers, waiting staff, sommeliers, as well as people on reception and covering reservations. That much was simple, but the devil was in the detail. From there, he would work out the number of bodies required, mapping it out from the top (him) down. The goo-goos were ranked by their abilities, ranging from 100 per cent goo-goo (a very blunt tool in the box) to a 20 per cent goo-goo (sharp at times). With a chilled cola and a smouldering ashtray at his side, George could be heard muttering to himself in a whisper, 'Okay, I've got a 40 per cent goo-goo and a 60 per cent goo-goo, so I need four more goo-goos on that section …' This unique system enabled members of staff to work in all the different sections. So, for instance, the commis with good English could be put on reception for a week, and a receptionist could be moved to work behind the bar for a while. Every individual would be able to play to their strengths, no matter what those strengths might be. He never got the rota wrong. Everything ran smoothly. For years I have done my rota in a similar way, on a massive piece of paper, which enabled me to see, at a glance, who would be doing what, where and when.

The key to a good rota, I believe, is to be like a football manager who is devising a team sheet. The team sheet sticks to the same format, but also changes for each match, depending on the team, what shape each player is in, and the team they are due to face on the pitch. You only compile your team sheet on the Friday night or Saturday morning, according to the opponents you are facing. It is similar for the manager in a restaurant. He needs to know who he is playing against (the number of covers, for instance), and what kind of players you have that day. Are they coming back from injury? Have they worked in the restaurant a long time and, therefore, are experienced? Do they understand the job? What weaknesses do they have? If they have weaknesses, are there specifics that need to be worked on? How can they be supported? Remember, really, there are no bad staff; there is just bad management. It is better to have bad staff than no staff. A good manager can work with bad staff if he manages the rota carefully.

———◄≡

A steady stream of visitors came through the door to see George, asking for favours, money, or simply a chat. Everyone respected George, and he was a pleasure to work with; there was never a dull day. Yes, he could get moody, but that may have been because he worked so hard and such long hours.

George seemed to believe that he owned the restaurant. Indeed, from what I could work out, it was George who made all the decisions. He did not really care about the big bosses. Every year there was a presentation to Conran's accountants, finance directors and executives. The idea was to deliver a speech about the restaurant, its sales, marketing and so on. Before heading off to do his presentation, I asked George what he intended to say. 'I've really thought it through,' he replied with certainty. 'I'm going to say, "I don't do presentations. But let me tell you about how I work. I am like Ronaldo. The team plays around me. They give me the ball and I score." So that's what I'll say to them. And then I'll say, "That's my presentation, thank you."'

I was not convinced, but off he went. At the meeting, George delivered his 'presentation' just as he said he would. There was a pause as the bosses looked at him with some trepidation. Then one of them, continuing the football analogy, said, 'So, George, tell me what happens if Ronaldo gets injured and can't play. Who will the ball be passed to? And who will score?' George did not really have the answers to those questions. He simply could not imagine the restaurant without him, the captain of the good ship Sartoria. 'In one week,' added the executive, 'I want your presentation.'

But the thing is, George was never injured, never took time off sick and he rarely took a holiday. He was there, fully in charge, from nine in the morning until one o'clock the following morning, and so was I. The only day he did not work was Sundays – that is when I was allowed to run Sartoria by myself. Although on those days I still had to phone him, just to reassure him that everything was running smoothly.

George's affection for goo-goos was infectious. Later on in my career I would come to adopt his goo-goo philosophy and work with them as if they were characters in a playstation game. I imagine that I have a controller in my hands and am directing the goos-goos. They all have certain levels, depending on their abilities. I can move them left and right, and up and down. 'Go to table six, take the order... clear table eight'. The trick is not to overload them, to give them only one job at a time. As with managing any team, it is about understanding everyone's strengths and weaknesses, and working hard to balance them. That way you know that the customer will have the best possible experience.

21

DODGY CHARACTERS
AND CLUB NIGHTS

In this business there are mavericks like George who run things differently but brilliantly, and then there are mavericks who are out for themselves and only themselves. Don was definitely the latter. He had started out as a waiter, working in a variety of smart hotels and restaurants, until finally settling in as the head sommelier of a upmarket hotel in London. He had an impressive knowledge of wine and a reassuring smile. He was trusted by both the guests and the management of the hotel. What none of them knew was that Don not only suggested and served the wines, but – behind the scenes – he drank them, too.

Don's illicit drinking really took off around the year 2000, when many wine producers began to use screw caps instead of corks. Screw caps prevent the wine from being 'corked' – when mustiness caused by a tainted cork renders the wine undrinkable. It only arises in bottles with corks, of course, and studies suggest that only about five out of 100 bottles are corked. But still, if an expensive bottle of wine is corked, and the guest rejects the wine, there is no guarantee that the wine supplier will refund the cost of the wine to the restaurant. That's the case for screw caps, but there are some disadvantages too. Many people agree that the taste buds are aroused by the sound and sight of a cork being pulled from a bottle. Then there is the ritual of touching and smelling the cork, as well as the enjoyment of seeing it on the table, beside the wine that you have chosen. The cork says Old World; the screw cap says New World. When it comes to pleasurable aesthetics, the screw cap is no match for the cork.

But when it comes to sommeliers with dodgy morals, the screw top is by far the best option. The temperature-controlled wine cellar of the restaurant where Don worked was lined with hundreds of unopened bottles, lying on their sides in racks along the walls. Now, if he fancied a glass of wine from a bottle with a cork, he would need to open the bottle and pour himself a glass, and would then have to push the cork back into the bottle. If any of his junior sommeliers walked into the wine cellar it would not take them long to spot the odd one out; rows and rows of unopened bottles would only serve to emphasise the single, open bottle.

But with screw tops, he was able to drink what he wanted, undetected. As head sommelier, Don decided which wines appeared on the wine list, and so was able to add a particular Australian white wine, with a screw cap closure. This Australian wine became his tipple during working hours. He could open it, help himself, screw the cap on and slide the bottle back into the rack – no protruding cork to give him away.

But in order to keep this up, he needed to stop his guests from ordering that particular wine. Imagine if someone had said to a junior sommelier, 'I'd like a bottle of the Australian so-and-so,' pointing to Don's wine, and the junior went to fetch the wine from the cellar and noticed that the bottle had been opened. Don's light-fingered, heavy-drinking habits would be exposed. So he told his juniors that it was not a wine to recommend, and his team obeyed the command. He even went so far as to dissuade guests from ordering it, and would suggest a different choice. He did not really want anyone else dipping into his supplies. 'It's okay,' he would say of the wine he was drinking bottles of daily. 'But may I recommend this Chablis, which, I might add, does not have a screw cap, which of course makes it higher quality. It's a very interesting wine, with a nose of plums and peaches … A subtle complexity and mineral thread …' Job done.

Don, meanwhile, continued on his extremely merry way, barely weaving or slurring as he went. There's more. At times, he kept a large bottle of Coca-Cola on ice, which was just for him. The contents of that bottle included a substantial amount of Jack Daniels. Come his retirement party, Champagne corks popped – no screw caps – and the hotel's general manager praised Don for his many years of commitment and integrity. 'Please join me in raising a glass to Don. When it comes to wine, he can always be trusted …' If only he knew!

Don is not alone; theft is rife in this profession. As long as there is cash in restaurants, some of it will disappear. Now that payment cards are used far more frequently than cash, it is harder to pull off, but it definitely happens. Booze, too, as the story of Don demonstrates. There are plenty of other stories, like the restaurant manager who opened a bottle of Bollinger every night before service. He would put the bottle of Champagne in the ice bucket, which was close to the waiters' station, out of sight from the guests at their tables. Every now and again the manager would swoop over to the waiters' station, pour himself a glass of Bolly and drink it quickly before returning to the floor. By the end of service, he would have drunk two bottles of Bollinger and at least £100 in profit. Then there was the restaurateur who was fully aware that members of his staff were taking beer and spirits from the bar – he just did not know who was responsible. He put in CCTV cameras, training them on the drinks in question. When he came to rerun the CCTV footage there were a few seconds when the screen went black before resuming its surveillance. This was because the staff switched off the lights, pinched the bottles, and then turned the lights back on. I have heard similar stories in which the camera lenses were momentarily covered with linen napkins while the alcohol was swiped. Restaurateurs can install clever spy cameras and CCTV above and beside tills, wine fridges, cupboards and larders, but all this makes no difference – stuff will still be taken. There are many fancy high-tech methods of monitoring stock and charting its movement. Stock is stolen nevertheless. In this business people have always stolen from their bosses.

When I was a teenage waiter at the Sporting Club in Monaco I had witnessed theft on a grand scale – even if it was merely the theft of cutlery (in particular, spoons). Taking something from a restaurant was regarded – and still is – as one of the perks of the job. Don would have thought, 'I work hard and I work long hours, the pay isn't great and therefore I deserve a little something in return.' Others tell themselves the same thing. Silver cutlery has always been a favourite. Staff are drawn like magpies to the glint of forks, knives and spoons. If you are one of those people who likes to pop an item of cutlery into your pocket or handbag, then do not imagine for one moment that it has not already been eyed up by your waiter or waitress.

Plates, too, are swiped by waiters, waitresses and chefs who want to fill their kitchen cupboards at home. In the past I have been invited to parties at colleagues' homes where I have found myself drinking and eating from glasses and plates that were distinctly familiar – and that is because they are the same as those used in the restaurant where we worked. I have known of restaurateurs who arrive in the morning and are horrified as they step into dining room – where there were ten tables and 40 chairs last night, there are now nine tables and 36 chairs. Some swine on the payroll has pinched the furniture and done a runner!

———⬱

Let's go back to the autumn of 2003. While the Black Eyed Peas were at the top of the charts (with *Where is the Love?*), and Concorde was making its last commercial flight, I was on my way to Noble Rot. A restaurant, with a private club and bar downstairs for members, Noble Rot was located on Mill Street, Mayfair, and was owned by Søren Jessen.

Søren is an interesting character. He was born and raised in Denmark where his friends included members of the royal family, and he liked to play polo. In the late 1990s he was a highly accomplished banker – he had held executive roles at Goldman Sachs and UBS – and then, one day, he strolled into an old banking hall in Lombard Street, in the City of London. 'This building should be a restaurant,' he thought, and he had the means to make his dream come true

Thereupon two things happened: first, the establishment of 1 Lombard Street, a restaurant which was immediately successful and is still going strong to this day with a Michelin star; and second, Søren's career as a restaurateur.

By October 2003, Søren had already acquired 3 Mill Street and transformed it in to Noble Rot. Noble Rot is the name given to the type of fungus (Botrytis) that affects grapes, but with beneficial effects, and can result in the most perfectly sweet wines. I think that for the wealthy Søren, Noble Rot was a playground as sweet as Sauternes. For me, it was a place to make my mark after Sartoria, and I certainly had my work cut out.

The ground floor restaurant was quite small, serving about 60 covers of exceptionally good food, including mushroom lasagne, which was divine, and quality meats like a beautiful rib-eye steak on the bone. Downstairs there was the members' club, with a bar, large enough for 120 people. The food may have been great, but there was a big problem. The entire place was 'run' without the slightest hint of discipline. The staff did whatever they wanted. I began as restaurant manager but very quickly became the general manager, which meant I oversaw the restaurant but also the club downstairs. It made sense that I should look after both so that I could make sure that everyone was doing what he or she was supposed to do.

Now, bar, clubs and restaurants are entirely different entities.

You might be able to run a restaurant very well, but it does not follow that you can run a wine bar or a club. And vice versa. The staff consisted of lots of goo-goos, as King George of Sartoria would have called them. My management style – namely to instil proper discipline – worked eventually, but it was a long, difficult journey. When I started, the team was very unwilling to change, and that was understandable: why would you want to do a good job when you could just do what you liked? There were a lot of staff who were drinking on the job and taking drugs.

There were some real characters, too, like, Tom, a waiter whose brother was a fellow GM. Tom was a heavy chap, due to his regular consumption of beer and junk food. One morning, before the doors opened, I noticed him standing near the bar, with his head in his hands and crying his eyes out. I did not want to intrude on his grief, but as his boss, I was concerned. Had a romance ended or, worse, had he lost a relative? 'Tom, are you okay?' I asked gently. 'What happened? Tom, do you want to tell me?' He raised his head and looked up at me – I can still see those chubby, tear-drenched cheeks – and said, 'Chelsea lost.' This was not, unfortunately, a one-off. In time I would come to realise that, just as the moon decides the tides, so, too, Tom's moods were determined by the performance of Chelsea FC on the pitch. I took to studying the upcoming football fixtures, to see who Chelsea were playing and whether I should expect to see a sobbing Tom. When the team beat Leeds 5-0, Tom was ecstatic. But when I heard the news that Manchester United had beaten Chelsea in the FA Cup semi-final, I knew to expect a broken-hearted Tom in work the next morning.

Like so many of his staff, Søren treated Noble Rot like a playground – and why not? He was a magnificent host, throwing parties for his large circle of friends, which included hedonistic socialites such as the late Tara Palmer-Tompkinson. His parties often went on until 5am, at which point the charming host would announce, 'All back to mine.' And he and his guests would head off to his home, while I contemplated the clear-up. He spent money on Noble Rot, too, but perhaps not as much as he should have done, and I always felt it could have been more of a success. It always felt a bit makeshift: the toilet doors, for instance, were always broken, and there was often a problem with the loos flushing, or rather, not flushing. There was also a flimsiness to the furniture, something you only noticed over time. It didn't quite fit with what the place was trying to achieve.

However, the flimsy furniture would fade into insignificance when compared to to his next venture. Let me be clear, Søren is a wise man with an astute financial brain, but the decision to buy Graze, his next place, was a huge mistake. As I had been successful with Noble Rot, Søren thought I could turn things around at Graze, which was a restaurant and a bar without a nightclub licence, in Maida Vale. It was called Graze because the food consisted of a sort of tapas-inspired modern European menu. The message was: come and graze here. But the food was not particularly good, and there were numerous menus, with more menus for cocktails and wine – enough to confuse the hell out of any guest. In addition, there was a noticeable lack of co-ordination in service due to a total breakdown in communication between the kitchen and the front of house. Well, I sorted that out pretty quickly, bringing in a chef called

Tom Cenci who had been at Noble Rot with me. Tom brought along his colleague and friend Dan Doherty, who would go on to become the head chef at Duck and Waffle in the City. Pretty soon, the old confusing menus had gone, and they had introduced one simple, clear menu. We were on our way to a strong team, but there were other hills to climb before we got there.

When Søren bought the place, there were regular DJ nights, but as these brought in the wrong sort of clientele – aggressive types, who wanted fights and drugs instead of beautiful tapas – we had to stop them. There were no more fights, of course, but we were left with even fewer customers than before. Now, this would have been a problem for any restaurant, but at Graze there were at least ten different hands in the till and stock was being stolen every day. The business was losing thousands of pounds every week.

At first, I did not know how much was being stolen, and who was stealing it. I could see, for instance, that a huge amount of spirits were going missing. But who was taking them? Soon, the truth emerged. A few members of the bar staff made frequent trips, from behind the bar to the back door, and then to the bins outside. Now, there is nothing unusual about carrying out clanking bin bags, but some of these bags contained bottles that were full rather than empty. These were collected by the bar manager when he finished work late at night, and kept for the bar staff's own enjoyment. When I told the bosses and suggested he should be sacked, they said, 'Okay. Hold on. There are procedures to follow. First, you'll have to let HR know. He has employment rights …' I was having none of that. He was stealing, pure and simple. The bar manager – and his team – had to go. If I wasn't allowed to fire him straight off then I had to find another way.

Late one night, as the restaurant was closing, I confronted the dishonest member of staff when he stepped through the back door, after yet another trip to the bins. 'You may as well go back outside.'

'Why?'

'Because you shouldn't work here anymore.'

'Why?'

'Because Scotland is having trouble trying to produce the amount of whisky you are nicking from us.'

We went outside to the bins, and started to go through them, pulling out the bags, one by one, untying them and looking inside at the contents. Bottle after bottle, filled to the brim with alcohol – whisky, gin, wine. He quit there and then because he realised I would never let it go.

———

With our new menu, superb food and a loyal staff who worked with – rather than against – each other, we soon became an operation that ran like clockwork. Everything would have been going brilliantly, if only we had had customers. It was down to location: Graze was situated right opposite a petrol station, not somewhere you would choose to take your wife or girlfriend on a date. And the people who did come to Graze tended not to graze, and usually drank nothing more expensive than Coca-Cola or orange juice.

We were left with no choice: if we wanted customers, we had to bring back the music. We met music promoters, found some cool DJs, and soon we were on our way back to success. The place was heaving and very soon we went from being thousands of pounds down to thousands of pounds up. I would love to end the story here, on a high note, but that was not to be.

Together with the large crowds came the return of the wrong sort of clientele and we noticed a lot more incidents of drug taking. Here's the thing about drugs: we all know that if people want to take drugs then they will take them. Security and other staff would check the toilets for people taking cocaine, but that is not as effective as making it difficult to take the stuff in the first place. These days, toilet cisterns are sloped to make it difficult to lay out lines of coke, and some clubs even remove the lids of the toilet seats. At Graze, before the days of the sloping cistern, we would rub a little bit of colourless oil (vegetable or sunflower would do) on top of the cistern. The coke would stick to the oil (that caused no damage to the cistern) and the drug instantly became unsnortable – job done.

There was one group of men that was very hard to deal with – both threatening and abusive. Although there were only 20 of them out of a crowd of 300, they always caused trouble, fights mainly, which meant we were forced to hire more security. I think they were proper gangsters and most of the time they seemed to have consumed large amounts of drink or drugs. Sometimes they would come in to the restaurant, and demand a table, almost roaring with rage. It was a surreal and stressful period. One night a man was stopped at the door and told he could not come in. He started mouthing off, and then began doing karate kicks – not hitting the doormen, but provoking them sufficiently to start a proper brawl. He was eventually ejected but it took three doormen to achieve it.

During this period, I took on a new security man to work with us. Zoran was a man mountain from the former Yugoslavia, who had learned combat in that country's equivalent of the SAS. His English was not always great, but he was fluent when he said to me, 'If you want me take anyone out, just say.'

'Zoran,' I said, 'thanks for the offer, but I don't want you to take anyone out.'

I had noticed – and you did not need to be especially observant to spot it – that many of our clientele wore baseball caps. As well as making them look like dealers straight out of the projects, the caps prevented their faces from being captured by CCTV cameras. If there was any trouble, we had difficulty identifying them. We therefore introduced a no hats policy in the club, to reduce our problems. I went to the man monster and said, 'Zoran, do not let anyone in who is wearing a hat.'

'No problem, Fred. No hats.'

This system seemed to work well for a couple of hours. Then, when I was dealing with guests in a corner of the room, I saw a commotion by the door. It looked like Zoran was about to take someone out. As I quickly moved towards the door, I could see what was happening – Zoran was forcibly trying to remove the skull cap from a Jewish man.

Zoran barked, 'Take off your hat! The manager says no hats.'

I squeezed in between the two men, saying, 'Zoran, please, please. It's a religious thing …'.

I apologised to the gentleman and he was allowed to wear his skull cap, but Zoran remained puzzled – he couldn't understand why the man was allowed to wear his hat – and again offered, 'If you want me to take him out, just say.'

This foray into club nights also gave me my first experience of club promoters – the guys that bring you a crowd. All dealings were in cash and the promoter usually took up to half the door takings. Now, that meant that I could have taken a large amount of the remaining half, and nobody would have known. I never did that, but it made me realise how businesses can lose money. When things are done in cash, it is oh so easy to put your hand in the till.

There were two particularly fierce girls who I remember. They were supposed to bring in a crowd but at the end of one particular night, they had brought in no one. As the last people left at 4am, these two promoters were still hovering around. One of them said, 'Can we have our money?'

I said, 'Well, hang on. You are paid 10 per cent when you deliver. And tonight you did not deliver, so I am not going to pay you.'

I must have said the wrong thing because one of the girls went bit crazy and started threatening me: 'Man, what are you talking about! I'm gonna get my bruv and he's gonna beat you up.' In the end I gave them some money just to shut them up. It was nowhere near 10 per cent of the takings, but they were lucky to get anything. They left and I never worked with them again. In fact, in the end, the promoters, the brawls and the aggression became too much. We stopped the music nights and, predictably, the business spiralled. Then it was shut – put out to graze.

22

—≡

TIPPING

I once worked in a restaurant where I was asked to arrange a special evening for a guest. He was a wealthy man, but he did not want a flashy extravaganza for a couple of hundred people. Instead, it was just a table for two – he and his wife. Somebody from his office – a chauffeur or bodyguard – came to the restaurant first to organise the evening: where they would sit, what they would have to eat and drink, and so on. He also mentioned that they would not be paying the bill in person, but that he would pay it later, and therefore they should not be presented with one.

The evening arrived, the couple sat down at their romantic table for two, and were just like any other guests. They had a wonderful time and, a few hours later, were happy when they left. As had been arranged with the chauffeur, they were not presented with a bill. Next, the chauffeur reappeared. He paid the bill and handed me an envelope. 'Here you are, this is for you.' Inside, there was a healthy wad of £50 notes. In fact it was £1,000 – three times larger than the bill for the meal. I would have been so happy and grateful with a just a thank you.

Alain Sourzac, my teacher at catering college, had liked to use the French proverb: 'Qui peut le plus, peut le moins.' He who can do the most, can do the least. By this, he would have also been referring to the money that can be made from gratuities – you tend to come across the top tippers in the top restaurants. But tipping these days is a minefield, whether you are paying the normal amount or something extraordinary. As I mentioned in an earlier chapter, in the old days it was clear what a tip was: a tip is over and above what you pay on the bill. In France, we say that the tip is 'pour boire' – for a drink. You hand over some money, saying, 'Thank you, and here's a little something for a drink.' People get tips in all sorts of jobs. My father even got tips when he worked as a nurse.

In restaurants, traditionally, the bill was presented and the guest either tipped or did not tip. The tip depended on the quality of service, and also was proportionate to the guest's kindness – was he generous or miserly? It would generally be cash. Even then, tips and service charge were a source of fierce discussion. When I was at catering college I would argue with fellow 16-year-olds about who should get the tip – the chef or the waiter? That was the extent of our debate. When I first came to London in 1992 that was the year in which tips became taxable. Until then, waiting staff were not required to pay tax on tips and so, if someone gave you a tenner, you could pop it in your pocket. Or the tips were put into a box and at the end of the month, or at the end of the week, the restaurant manager shared out the cash. He would use the point system: eight points for the head waiter, one point for the commis, and so on ... And it was tax free. But, after 1992 this was no longer the case.

Then the service charge came along. This is a more tax efficient system where the recipient does not pay National Insurance on this sort of income. However, there are some points of contention concerning what the law says about service charge, and how service charge is interpreted from one restaurant to another. The service charge is not applied consistently across the country, and consequently there is no clarity for the millions of people who eat out every day and gaze at the bill, wondering, 'What is the service charge? What should it be? Does it go to the staff? Or do the management or the owner take it?' The charge is often described on the bill as 'discretionary' or 'optional', which only adds to the confusion. Legally, as a customer, you do not have to pay the service charge. So as the guest, you might be thinking, 'I do not want to pay the service charge because I'm not sure who'll receive it, but I do want to leave a tip for the waiter, so what do I do?'

Well, here's my view. Think of a restaurant, and the people who work there. Now all you have to do is ask yourself: who should receive a cut of the service charge? The waiter should get some of it, of course. Who can argue with that? But then, he cannot serve the food if it is not cooked. So surely the chef should also receive part of the service charge, shouldn't he? But hang on, if the chef receives something, what about the kitchen apprentice? He has also made a contribution. And the cutlery and plates were clean, weren't they? So what about the kitchen porter? What about the girl at reception? She has played a part, hasn't she? And what about the person who looks after the marketing, and who has brought in lots of guests? You cannot just give it to a few because there are so many more who are also doing very valuable work. You may not see them, but they are still part of the operation.

Let's say a booking is done well for a special event. It's a birthday party and the guest wants Champagne and it is delivered by the waiter, but actually, the waiter only knew about it because the reservations team were diligent and wrote down the request. How could you not give the reservations team some of the service charge, and acknowledge their contribution? But the guests at the party only see the waiter who brings the Champagne, and they therefore might want to give him £10, £20 or £50, without realising the efforts of the team behind him. As a customer you must always remember that the waiter is like the anchor leg in the relay race: there might be four people on the team but the runner who gets the cheers and applause is the one who crosses the finishing line. He might have won the race but could he have done so without the help of the other three? Of course the answer is 'No'. Every restaurant works in a slightly different way, so it would be impossible to dictate a mandatory split. However, I do think it is crucial to understand that there are different ways of viewing the industry, and acknowledging who actually contributes to the experience of a guest.

There is an established way of dealing with this issue, the *tronc* system. The word *tronc* comes from the French word for a collection box, used to raise a bit of money during a church service, or cash for the poor. Under the tronc system, all takings from the service charge go into a specially designated account, also known as the tronc. This is looked after, not by the management or accountant for the company, but by a 'troncmaster', who is on the staff, or it is overseen by a group of employees. They have a points system, and the restaurant employees are awarded points – the more points they have, the greater their share of the gratuities, drawn from the tronc. The troncmaster of each restaurant must ask himself the sort of questions I have asked above. Who deserves what? Who contributes? One establishment might awards points to everyone, while another might award points to only the kitchen brigade and front of house, and another might share the entire tronc among the waiting staff, and no one else gets a bean.

The tronc can work well, and would be perfect if customers were given a clear view of service charge and where it might be going to within the tronc. But as we don't share that with customers, over the years I have heard many guests say, 'I don't want to pay the service charge because I want it to go to you, so I will leave it as a tip.' Now, let's say the bill is £100 and there is 12.5 per cent service, giving a total of £112.50. The guest pays £100 but when it comes to the tip, they give you only £5. They may believe this is the correct amount to give, but of course it only acknowledges one person in the chain. By paying that fiver, the customers are ignoring the others who have contributed to the meal that has just been cooked for and served to them. Plus, the reason the service charge is £12.50 (and not £5) might be because it goes directly to contribute to the incomes of the staff. The restaurant pays between 40 and 70 per cent of a waiter's income. The rest is made up from what is in the tronc. So if you don't put any money in the tronc, there is no money there to pay that waiter. And if, as the guest, you give £5 instead of £10, then you are only giving him 50 per cent of his earnings, yet you may also believe that everybody should be paid.

To avoid these sorts of issues, there are those who say that the service charge should be included on the bill, so that it is part of the whole sum and not optional. Therefore, instead of being a bill of £100 with a discretionary service charge of £12.50, the bill becomes £112.50. However, if that were to happen, the service charge would have to go through the restaurant's account, meaning that National Insurance would have to be paid on it by the staff and they would end up with less money in their pocket.

I think there should be a system whereby we have a service charge which is entirely tax-free income for the restaurant staff. It would not be discretionary, but a compulsory charge, rather like VAT or indeed the cost of the meal itself. With a compulsory, tax-free charge, the wages of waiters would increase. We need to see a few benefits in this profession. A system like this could bring many positive changes: it would save money for restaurant owners; with higher wages, staff would do a better job; more people would be drawn to the industry; the perception of the industry would change for the better; service would improve even further and ultimately business would grow.

23

CHEFS AND WAITERS

When I started out in this profession, and even until quite recently, bullying and abuse were common in restaurants. When the chef yelled – for whatever reason – everybody shut up. 'You don't argue with the chef,' was the number-one rule. And people most didn't. For a waiter, as the chef was on the other side of the pass, he was allowed to have his outburst of anger and get away with it. But in fact the pass offered no real protection and waiters still got it in the neck from the chef. And on the other side, the chef's chefs got it in the neck – or any part of their body that took his fancy.

I have worked in establishments where the head chef, no matter how talented at the stove, could suddenly lose it. Crash! A plate would be thrown on the floor, or against the wall. He would swear at a chef in his brigade, or at a waiter who was waiting, tray in hands; at that moment anyone close by was in danger. This is how one man's madness can and does define the culture of a restaurant.

The aggression, abuse and violence would spread through the ranks, and across the pass. It was chefs on chefs and also chefs on waiters and, at times, it was pretty intense. Employment laws have helped to change things, and thankfully the younger generation abhors the abuse and violence that for so long was the ugly side of the industry. It did not happen all the time, I have to say, but when the stress became too much, then the trouble, yelling and plate-throwing was always seconds away.

I am sure that none of this will come as news to you. These sorts of kitchen dramas are well documented in books, newspapers and magazines. Many accomplished chefs, who are now also successful restaurateurs, have spoken about their past 'leadership' styles and publicly regret their behaviour in the kitchen.

But it is not entirely a thing of the past. The trouble arises when there is a loose cannon, often the head chef or an idiot of a manager, or you might be in an establishment where there is not just one, but a few fools in the kitchen. They can cook, and that is about it, but they are aggressive, unfriendly, uncooperative, and they are not customer-focused. Instead, the focus is on them, the aggressive chefs, and what they can cook and how macho they are. The smallest question receives a hostile response: 'Yeah! Waddya want!'

As a member of staff, you either put up with it or you move to another restaurant. Quite frankly, I am not here to be told to go away or to be sworn at, no matter who the chef on the other side of the pass is. Over the years this has resulted in a number of Mexican stand-offs. There is always the tendency to try and justify this sort of belligerent behaviour. 'He's a gifted chef and a hardworking man, but okay, he's also a bit of a psycho, so you've gotta take it.' Well, I just don't accept that reasoning. In a restaurant, everyone needs to work together. If you are rude and aggressive, you prevent that from happening, and no matter how good you are, if you get in the way of that, then you are out.

Aggression aside, there has always been an age-old battle between chefs and waiters. Traditionally, they do not get along very well. These days, chefs and waiters do mix, but generally, when the staff of a restaurant hit the pub after service, you tend to see chefs congregating in one corner and waiters in another.

Now, though I never let the divide get in the way, and have some close friends who are chefs, I must say I have come across some particularly choice chefs in my time. And by 'choice', in some cases I mean filthy, literally filthy. I remember I was once in a kitchen talking to a chef who was in the middle of preparing about 25 pigeons. To do this the chef had to squeeze his fingers into each bird to remove its gizzards. His hands were soaked in blood and guts and, as I stood there, he suddenly ran his fingers through his long hair, pushing it back from his face. Now his hair and forehead were drenched in the stuff as well as his hands. I said, 'Man, look at yourself. You can't do that. Do you know anything about hygiene?'

And just as there are waiters who cannot serve, not all chefs have a palate and not all chefs can even cook. I remember an occasion when I asked the chef to make me a dish of smoked chicken salad, which was served with a poached duck egg. When the dish arrived I cut into the egg, popped a sliver into my mouth and discovered … the egg was stone cold. It had been poached earlier on in the day, which was fine, but the chef had failed to heat it through in boiling water before serving it.

I went into the kitchen and said, 'What is going on? This egg is cold.' I was not the only one to have received a cold egg. Every guest who ordered this dish was also given a cold poached egg. This is a very basic thing to get right, and yet it was wrong. Every part of a guest's restaurant experience must make them go, 'Wow!' A cold egg doesn't quite do it. The chef in charge of poaching the eggs had not finished off the process, and the head chef had not spotted this error at the pass, before the plates left the kitchen. No one had checked.

As you know, my experience of food is deeply rooted. At the age of two, I was eating coq au vin cooked by my mother. There were frequent dinner parties chez Sirieix. I'm a trained chef, and I have worked in fantastic places and eaten beautiful food. All this knowledge means I question what I eat: does this mouthful taste as good as it possibly could? Does it need a touch more butter? A touch more salt? I am astonished by the inability of some chefs to question themselves in the same way, to analyse what they are tasting and whether it tastes right.

I remember working in a restaurant where the chef cooked a dish of red mullet with agrodolce sauce. He wanted to put it on the menu. This sauce is made from vinegar and sugar, and should have a sweet and sour taste – the name comes from the Italian *agro* (sour) and *dolce* (sweet). But it was so agro that it was like eating vinegar. It was one of the most disgusting sauces I have ever tasted, and yet the chef proudly believed with all his heart that his red mullet with agro (I won't even mention dolce) sauce was excellent. He did not take the criticism well, but the guests were spared this dish.

There are also times when chefs do not seem to appreciate that everything we do – our role, our mission – is always for the enjoyment of the guests. A guest might say of a dish, 'It's not good ... Too much salt,' or, 'There's not enough sauce.' I might agree. And the chef might agree. But they will still go into a strop: 'Yeah, well you tell them that they can stick their dish ...'

They simply do not understand the way it works, out there on the floor, where we are face to face with the guest who is paying all our wages. Let's face it, if you cook a dish and it is not well received, then what are you going to do? Leave the kitchen, go into the dining room and argue with the guest? You never argue with the guest, especially not when he or she is grumbling about too much salt in a sauce.

This might seem obvious, but I have worked with chefs who have a serious problem with this. They regard any negative comments as critiques of their food, and of their hard work. They take it to heart – a personal insult. But this is madness: if the customer is not happy, then none of us have done our jobs properly, and there should be less salt in the dish.

At Galvin at Windows, I review every new dish for the menu. If I do not give it the thumbs-up, then it is back to square one, and the dish is either dropped or refined. If a sauce is too oily, for instance, the recipe will be adjusted so that our food is consistently good and the best is being served to the guest at the outset, rather than being adapted after criticism (or even complaints) from the guests. When I taste new dishes,

I look at them not from a chef's perspective, or even my own perspective, but from the customer's perspective. I ask myself, 'Is this an amazing dish? Does it match our vision to give an amazing experience to each guest? Will I, the guest, be bowled over by it?' We internalise the process of criticism and feedback as much as possible, so that everyone on both sides of the pass is completely happy with everything that goes out. Thus, in a way, this should not be regarded as criticism but rather as part of the process of creation. I know what you might be thinking, 'He gets to critique all the dishes but he doesn't cook any of them!' but I'm the guy on the front line, so I know what the customers want.

Although chefs are often regarded as as the violent members of the restaurant team, I have seen waiters with a nasty streak. As with the tricky chefs, I weed them out and get rid of them immediately. At Galvin at Windows we have a culture in which we behave respectfully and kindly towards each other. I certainly appreciate there is stress during service and I do not mind a bit of shouting from time to time, but there has to be a basic culture of respect and kindness.

There can be playful banter, too. Yesterday I heard about a kitchen in London where the chef is forever talking about his sex life and the size of his manhood. He brought Viagra pills into the kitchen and was showing them off to the brigade. He offered one to his sous chef, 'Does you want one?' 'Erm, no, a kind offer but ...' I don't think he took him up on the offer but as he waved the packet around, one of the tablets fell into a bowl filled with the chefs' tasting spoons. Everything was thoroughly washed and there were never any complaints from the male guests in the room ...

———✦———

Boxing is my other life; I have already talked about how it compares with service and how this has helped me in my job. In some ways, my charity boxing match with Marcus Wareing in 2012 turned all of this into reality. My intention was to raise money for Galvin's Chance, an initiative I started at Galvin at Windows with Chris Galvin and the DM Thomas Foundation in 2008, to help disadvantaged young people get into training, education and full-time employment in front of house in the best hotels, restaurants and bars in London. By 2012 fundraising was becoming increasingly difficult, so I organised a star-studded boxing tournament called Rumble in the Kitchen. Tickets sold out in two weeks and we made £55,000 for the charity in one night.

It was a white-collar boxing tournament, with Marcus and I at the top of the bill. There were 20 other contestants, almost all of them from the hospitality industry. In order to persuade Marcus to compete in the event, I went to see him at his kitchen in the Berkeley Hotel, off Knightsbridge. I told him a bit about the tournament, and then said, 'Hey Marcus, do you want to fight me?' His reply? 'You're going to hospital, mate.'

I smiled, but I was determined that, come the night of the big fight, I would knock him out. And for the whole bout I really hated him: three rounds of two minutes, all in the name of charity and entertainment.

Marcus had considerable experience in the ring. As a lad growing up in Southport, Merseyside, he was not into team sports. Instead, he boxed. Boxing helped to keep him focused. When he came to London in 1988, to work in the kitchens of

The Savoy, he stayed at digs in Earl's Court. He worked hard and was a loner without a social life. He did not go out drinking in pubs or clubs, or spend his money on clothes and cigarettes. He saved his money and spent his limited free time in the gym, where he boxed. Me? I'd taken up boxing a few years before. I had nothing like his experience, but I did have passion.

Early bouts on the night included one between a pair of waiters from Hawksmoor and another between Hayden Groves, executive chef at hospitality provider BaxterStorey, and Paulo de Tarso, senior maître d' from Bar Boulud at the Mandarin Oriental. To add to the fun, each of us had been given a boxer-style nickname. I was Sugar Fred, 'The Stinger', up against Marcus 'The Hitman' Wareing. Monica 'The Hacker' Galetti, at that time senior sous chef at Le Gavroche, fought TV presenter Penny 'The Mighty' Mallory. Monica won.

Marcus was already waiting in the ring when I marched towards him. At his side was his brother, who had come along as Marcus's corner man. 'My' music was blaring. It was AC/DC's 'Fire Your Guns'. In my corner I was surrounded by some of the stars of the TV show Gladiators who had turned up – in their colourful, body-hugging outfits – to support me. I was on a high; the adrenaline was coursing through my body and, it seemed, through the entire room. I was raring to go. Eager to fight. Ready to win.

I think I was stronger and fitter than Marcus, but when the first bell sounded I came out of my corner like a madman. I rushed in and threw the kitchen sink at him. Even though I am no good at fighting at close range, I attempted to go toe-to-toe. I failed to stick to my game plan. I wanted to knock him out cold, but many of my shots missed the mark. Marcus just stood there, letting me waste my energy. By the second round, I was starting to flag, and when the bell rang at the end I didn't hear it and I kept on fighting. This created another drama: Marcus's brother jumped into the ring and there was a bit of pushing and shoving as he tried to make it clear that the bell had rung. Then my corner man leapt into the ring, and the two of them seemed to be squaring up. It was all good spirited fun, although I was slightly dazed and not quite sure exactly what was going on – and I was not the only one. In fact my corner man was so distracted that when he sent me out for the third round he forgot to put in my gum shield.

The final round was shambolic. At one point, Marcus and I sort of embraced each other and fell to the floor. Momentarily, we switched sports – from boxing on our feet to wrestling on the canvas. It was during this round that he broke his foot, admittedly, not the sort of injury that you would associate with boxing. A broken nose? Yes. Concussion? Possibly. A broken foot? No.

At the end of round three the final bell rang. As there had not been a knock-out, the winner was to be decided on points. 'And the winner is …' The room was hushed. '… MARCUS WAREING!'

His children came into the ring and helped to lift him up, as you do with the victor. Then he lifted my gloved hand into the air, and said, 'Well done, you gave me a good fight.'

Thankfully neither of us was seriously hurt. My father had travelled from France especially to see me fight. He was relieved, as you can imagine, that I had not suffered brain damage. For all my boxer's bravado, I had not really wanted to kill Marcus, of course. I did not hate him. And he did not want to put me in hospital – as it turned out, he put himself in hospital. While the rest of us went to a club and danced into the early hours of the following day, Marcus was in Accident and Emergency, receiving treatment for his broken foot. He remained in a cast for weeks afterwards. More recently, I emailed him to suggest a rematch, I received the response along the lines of, 'I'm too busy at the moment.' But perhaps after he has read this chapter, he'll be ready …

24

MAKING A RESTAURANT

In the spring of 2006, I received a call from Chris Galvin. He wanted to talk about a possible venture. Mighty oaks from little acorns grow, as they say. This call would lead, eventually, to the creation of Galvin at Windows, which sits on the twenty-eighth floor of the London Hilton in Mayfair. When Chris got in touch with me, the restaurant was little more than one month away from opening. One month! Chris had only signed his contract a few months earlier. The restaurant and bar needed a general manager – someone to oversee things. Chris, and the hotel's general manger, Michael Shepherd, were running out of time.

I went along for an interview. The floor-to-ceiling windows on every side of the room and bar provided unique and mesmerising views over London in all directions. In terms of what the guests would see from the tables, there was nothing like it in London. But the restaurant was a shell. Wires and cables were hanging from the ceilings, builders in hard hats were hard at work everywhere. It was dusty, and I had to tread carefully to avoid bumping into ladders or tripping over tools. A month or so from opening, and there was no hint of what the place was going to look like: there were supposed to be carpets, lighting and a huge, specially commissioned sculpture that was being shipped over from Milan to form a majestic centrepiece suspended from the ceiling. But at that moment, there was just dust.

They needed tables, chairs, crockery, cutlery and glassware; a fully-working kitchen with a substantial, well-trained brigade of chefs; and a large regiment of waiters and waitresses, trained to deliver the highest standards. In what was to be the bar they needed more tables and chairs, together with all the drinks a guest might ask for and tip-top bar staff. Above all there needed to be hundreds of guests having a fantastic time on the twenty-eighth floor.

I looked around, visualised what it would look like and how it would operate. I said, 'It's O.K. I can see how it will work. From here, I can see all of the restaurant. I can see the bar and the entrance. It's going to be easy to run. No problem.'

The job had my name written all over it. I could feel it. I had decided to take the post before they even offered it to me. I knew it would be hard: we had to move at breakneck speed and there were a million things to do. Life was stamped: 'URGENT!'

Before all that could begin I still had to serve out my notice period. I was the manager at Kilo (that had previously been Noble Rot) and I couldn't just leave. This meant that I had to find some way – any way – to prepare the launch of one restaurant while fulfilling my responsibilities and working at another. I owed it to Søren, who had always been good to me. Luckily, Kilo was on Mill Street, just a short stroll from the Hilton. And fortunately there are 24 hours in a day, otherwise I do not know how I would have done it.

So, at the crack of dawn, I would leave home and go to the Hilton. For the morning, I would be the general manager to Galvin at Windows, arguing with suppliers, making sure the tables were the right ones. A few hours later, I would go to Kilo, and oversee that restaurant. After lunch service, I would nip back to Galvin at Windows for a couple of hours. Then I would dash back to Kilo for evening service. When that was finished, I'd hurry back to the evolving shell in the skies.

Chris, meanwhile, was pulling together the kitchen, the brigade, and devising the menus. It was as if Chris and I had been parachuted behind enemy lines, with only one gun and one rucksack, and we were supposed to survive for four weeks. To add to all the challenges that faced us, we had the immense pressure of knowing that all eyes were on us. We were not merely opening a restaurant. We were opening the restaurant at the top of a legendary London landmark. This was no cheap bistro or café. It was a £2 million investment. We worked exhaustingly long hours, and I survived on very little sleep. However, I knew exactly what I had to do – everything would be okay, although I would have to work on convincing everyone around me. Whatever happened, I was going to win.

The Press, both national and international, was waiting and watching, as were people in our industry. Our so-called friends in the business always watch, you know. They wish you luck but secretly hope and pray that you'll fail – the usual schadenfreude. The clock was ticking, taking us closer to Judgement Day.

The space had previously been a restaurant. It had been Windows on the World, taking its name from the restaurant and bar at the top of the World Trade Center in Manhattan. Then, in the 9/11 terror attack on the Twin Towers, 54 members of the team lost their lives. As a mark of respect, the restaurant at the Hilton on Park Lane became Windows. I was to inherit the staff from its previous incarnation, which would present its own advantages, as well as, sadly, major headaches and difficulties.

No matter what business you are in, when there is change it is often not widely accepted or embraced. For many of the staff, my vision – and the way that I wanted to achieve it – was a total culture shock, and that's putting it mildly. Frequently, I was confronted by extreme reluctance to do things my way. Windows on the World had been run very differently. There was a morning team and there was a night team. You did your shift, then you went home. Not on my watch! I wanted 100 per cent commitment, discipline, hard work, long hours and precise attention to detail. Some staff were definitely not with me. They stuck to their own agenda. There was one person, for instance, who had worked in the old restaurant for quite a few years. He liked it just the way it was, and wanted it to remain exactly as it had been. I understood and sympathised with the sentiment, but I had a vision and a mission to accomplish. It had to be done my way if it was going to work, and I was not going to let go of or compromise my values for anyone.

One day, following a disagreement, we had a chat in my office. I said to him, 'Listen mate, it's not going to be like it was before. It just can't. This is a totally different business that just happens to be located on the same spot. That is all. The old way is gone forever and won't come back. The twenty-eighth floor has evolved and that's the way it is. So we need to embrace the change together. You are either in or out. What is it going to be?' He broke down in tears.

I said, 'Right. Just relax. Breathe, breathe, breathe … and think about what you want to do. What is important is that you enjoy what you do and do it for yourself. Okay?' I am so pleased to say that he stayed and became one of the key people responsible for the success of the business.

———━

As you know, there are no bad staff, only bad management. If you are a weak manager and let things go, you cannot set up a place like Galvin at Windows. Imagine, for example, you are a car manufacturer. You are Bentley and you've designed a Mulsanne, let's say, that has a very specific look. You go to the factory, the components come in and then the guys on the factory floor get involved.

And they tell you, 'Oh, it's nice but you know what? In terms of spec, we'd rather put Fiat wheels on it. It would better, it would be a bit edgy. And we'll have a Ferrari bonnet, a red one. It'll be lovely.' No one would buy it. It's not the brand. And the Galvin brand – this restaurant and bar – is very specific. Our vision and values were clear from the start when we knew exactly what we wanted to do. We wanted to give an amazing experience to each and every guest. We wanted to be one of the best restaurants in London, to set our mark, and to achieve this, you have to know what you are going to deliver and how you are going to do it.

The food, for example, is like a new design of car. It is relatively easy to deliver: there is a recipe. Everyone knows and understands that there is always a recipe for food. It can be improved and refined, but the recipe exists and just needs to be followed. However, most people do not have, or do not like to have a recipe for service. But I have one, and I know exactly what and how I want things done. My recipe was very hard for the staff to master, even though it was very simple.

As the manager, you know that you can only trust people when they do what they say they are going to do. Gradually, that trust will build. At this point you have a strong idea of who they are, as people. It takes time, after all, to get to know people. When I have explained something as clearly as I like to think I do, they get it. But if they don't get it, they ask questions. And if they ask questions, you can explain to them again until they do understand. Repetition is the key to training. I said, repetition is the key to training. Have you got it now?

———◀

A strong link between manager and staff is essential. In the movie *Avatar* the Na'vi are tall, yellow-eyed humanoids with long neural braids, similar in appearance to human hair, which provides an insight into their state of mind and is also used to form a neural connection with other living creatures on the planet. If a Na'vi starts riding a horse, for example, he is able to connect with the horse, and suddenly they become one being, yet the Na'vi remains in control. This is how I see the beginning of service. I have to make a neural connection with each and every member of staff. It sounds strange, but my point is that we have to be on the same wavelength. We operate as one being, but as the manager I am the one in control: it is my vision and my will, as well as my methods and standards, which will help us to deliver. I might be working with somebody who is only 10 per cent good, but still he knows what I want. We have a connection. I might be at a table taking an order, and when a waiter passes by I can ask him to do one thing, or even just nod towards a table, and he will read my signals. 'Clear the glasses from table seven.' When that is done, he will receive another task. As the manager, I need to be completely awake and aware.

When you watch a trapeze artist at the circus, you know that nothing can go wrong because he has a net, and during service a good manager acts as a net. He allows his staff to get on with their work, and if they fall – gasp! – it does not matter. They fall into the net, there is no harm done, no bones broken, and they can climb back up to the trapeze and carry on. The manager is there to protect the staff and to protect the guests.

We are completely focused on getting the job done, little by little, one task at a time, with no deviation. People, I have found over the years, enjoy that sort of focus and organisation. It brings job satisfaction. Time goes quickly and you get a great sense of achievement before, during and after service, and that sense of achievement is something you can't buy. But you can only get the job done if you have rigour and discipline; without these qualities, people become lazy and standards slip. I have seen it time and time again. People really do cherish discipline; when it exists, they become completely at one with what they are doing. When you feel immersed in a task and can see that you are working towards the same goal as your team, that feeling of fulfilment is unbeatable.

—◀≡

I often think of the floor – the dining room – as a stadium. You can see I am fond of comparing what we do to things that exist in the world outside the restaurant! As the general manager, I am, let's say, the midfielder on a football pitch. I can pass the ball here and there, to this person or that. I can set things up. I can race to defend or attack. I can be in the right place at the right time. I can co-ordinate and control, and manage and develop the other players. That's you, ladies and gentlemen.

My hope is that I can give you that burst of inspiration when you most need it. A good restaurant manager can make all the difference, just like Maradona did when he single-handedly won the World Cup in 1982. This is what I see on floor, and this is what the people – the guests – will see.

Every waiter is on his station. Or, if you like, his part of the pitch. If somebody attacks, I want one of my players there to defend. I want him to look at his team-mates, as well as the opposition – that's the guests – and, of course, to keep his eye on the ball, which is the guests being satisfied when they walk out of that front door, having enjoyed a few hours of escapism.

—◀≡

We opened Galvin at Windows on 16 May 2006, to acclaim from our customers and plaudits from the critics. Those first couple of weeks included a few Press events and there's one in particular that sticks in my mind. It was a sparkling affair, as waiters circulated with trays of Champagne and Mojitos for the guests. But three of the circulating waiters had devised a plan. They would return to the back of house with the trays – when most of the glasses were empty but some were still full – and there, out of sight, they would neck the contents of the full glasses. As the evening wore on, they became increasingly drunk. They were drunker than the guests.

This type of behaviour goes back to the belief held by some members of staff: 'I work very hard and long hours, therefore I am entitled to a few perks, such as free Champagne and Mojitos.' Actually, no. It's nothing more than theft. These guys were weaving all over the place. Two were dismissed that night. At four o'clock the following morning, the third was discovered by hotel security. He was paralytic and asleep by a lift, snoring loudly, on the seventeenth floor. He was helped out of the building and we never saw him again.

The rest of us, meanwhile, were sober and did not have time to drink or sleep. The train was still hurtling along, although now with plenty of passengers on board. We had to refine, perfect and scrutinise. The restaurant had been built, of course, but now we had to continue to build, and never stop. Build an image. Build a brand. Build a reputation – and maintain it. The stress does not go away. The 18-hour days continue, seven days a week, month after month. Chris, meanwhile, began to think about his next restaurant, Galvin La Chapelle. This would bring another layer of pressure to his life. One day, Chris and I were in Galvin at Windows when things got particularly tricky.

We were having a conversation at a table close to reception, and were discussing a guest who had complained about a bill.

The guest said he was apparently overcharged or that he was mis-sold a drink, because he was not made aware of the price. It was a brandy, at £250 for a glass. It was a concern, of course, but Chris seemed overly bothered about it, even though I assured him it would all right. He was, as I say, preoccupied by La Chapelle. Suddenly, he turned white with rage. He got to his feet, and he's a big man, much bigger than me. He yelled at me. 'Don't you tell me about my restaurant … Don't you ever tell me how to run my …' There was some colourful Anglo-Saxon language thrown in. I stood up too, he put his face close to mine and continued with his screaming.

I looked at him. 'You know what, Chris – I'm not taking this.' Then I stormed off. I had to get away. If I had stayed, either I was going to get punched or I was going to punch him. I went to my office, and sat down. But it was not over. Chris came in. 'Don't you walk away from me when I'm talking to you!'

I said, 'Chris, you can do whatever you like. You can tell me off. You can insult me. You can do all of that. But you can't be physically aggressive towards me. It's not on. I'm not taking it.' I stood up and walked away again.

It was the start of a particularly difficult period in my life. I had no idea how long it would last, but for two or three weeks I was furious and did not know what to do. I continued to work in a terrible atmosphere of uncertainty. But we had created this restaurant together, and we were in it for the long haul. I knew deep down that Chris was not an idiot, he was just very, very stressed. Restaurant life is never just about clinking Champagne glasses, Mojitos and smiles. Thankfully, we resolved our fight. We moved on. Our relationship has got stronger and stronger, and there is deep, mutual respect. I really admire Chris. He is not just a chef anymore; he's a businessman. Chris is a real inspiration and I will always remember two pieces of advice he has given to me. 'In life we can do whatever we want.' And 'You've got to be prepared to get the sack. If you can't do that you are no good.' I am laughing as I write this because in my time at Galvin at Windows I can definitely think of two or three times when I was this close to it. Since we opened the restaurant, Chris and I have travelled around the world together once or twice a year on inspiration trips. The aim is to return with ideas and recipes for the twenty-eighth floor. It's work but my God, do we have fun! Apart from the ideas and recipes, whatever happens on the trips stays on the trips.

———⋹

I always feel that if you meet the expectation of your guests then you have fulfilled your side of the bargain and people will come back. You have to strive to thrive. There is no time to rest on your laurels. Now, I must tell you, this is something I am always afraid of, especially here at Galvin at Windows. I am scared that I have missed something. What is it? What did I forget? Who didn't I say thank you to? Who didn't I remind to do a job? Am I late? Are my staff happy? Do I have enough guests? You have to think like this, if not, then apathy sets in and you start to go backwards.

After all, when you have finished a decent lunch, then it is time to contemplate your next feast. Now, where shall I go for dinner?

ACKNOWLEDGEMENTS

Thanks to Susannah Otter, Sarah Lavelle, Miranda Chadwick, Ed Griffiths, James Steen, Chris Galvin, Ken and Claudia Sanker, Pierre and Si Houy Lao-Sirieix, Michael Shepherd, Simon Vincent, Michel Roux Jnr, Emmeric Hurault, Shawana Williams, Michele Caggianese, Joëlle Marti and Andrew Sicklin for their help on this book.